FROM RUST TO TRUST

Peter's Tips for Living a Principle-Centered and Other-Focused Life

By Peter O'Dunne and David B. Glover

Printed by CreateSpace, An Amazon.com Company

www.createspace.com/5847776

ISBN: 978-1519791733

2/12/16

Dan,

I hope you enjoy the book and website.

Pete

This book is dedicated to Peter's family:
Kathy, Katie and Rudy.

Table of Contents

Peter's Acknowledgements

I am deeply grateful to so many who have made this book possible. Without you, I wouldn't have had the stories that I share in this book.

Cindy and Bill: Thank you for your patience and dedication over the past twenty-five years. Your ability to make right choices daily and your willingness to continually embrace change and improvement helped to build a business culture that will live on forever. You both live the principle-centered and other-focused life outlined in this book, and it's because of you that there is a legacy to pass along. I wish you both continued success and happiness. The very best is yet to come. Clarence would be so proud of you both.

Clarence: You are my friend and mentor forever. In so many ways, you lived your life for others: your family, your customers and even complete strangers. When I first met you, I was an introvert. You guided and influenced me to become an other-focused and principle-centered leader. You helped me to find and develop my gift. You had faith in me and gave me the opportunity to help so many others just as you did in your life. My life has been extraordinary because of knowing you.

Jon: Thanks for believing in me, inspiring me, and introducing me to the Ironman race. Our friendship means so much. I look forward to seeing you at my 80th birthday party.

David: Special thanks for your friendship and coaching. This book would not have been possible without your leadership, writing talent and vast experiences. Anything really is possible when you are principle-centered and other-focused. Our journey together has been memorable and significant. Thank you for openly sharing your stories and your life with the world and me. I am looking forward to our next steps together beyond the publishing of this book.

With deep gratitude, I acknowledge my family, Kathy and Katie, for their love and support.

Foreword

"What you leave behind is not what is engraved in stone monuments,
but what is woven into the lives of others."
~ Pericles ~

From Peter:

My father died when I was a sophomore in college, leaving me wishing I had the chance to have known him better. I wanted something from my dad that said, 'This is what I'm all about.' So this book is my story about what I'm all about that I can now share with my daughter, Katie, my wife, Kathy, my friends, my company, Mid-Atlantic Rubber and the strangers who read this book.

At its core, this book and the true stories in it are about the universal principles that can guide all of us: principles that can be applied to business, athletics, personal growth, family and friendships. Principles that help us move from rust to trust.

If I could summarize the "takeaways" of this book in a few key messages, they would be these:

Inside Out
Start with the core (principles, habits) and work outwards.

Upside Down
Leaders lead by serving others (not the other way around).

Backwards
Doing the right thing may mean doing the opposite of what everyone else is doing.

From David:

When Peter first approached me in 2010 to write a book for him, I was his triathlon coach. I had also written my own book about my experiences with triathlon, the Navy and being a cancer survivor. I began interviewing Peter with the intention to capture the stories about his company, Mid-Atlantic Rubber, as he began the transition away from his role as CEO after twenty years with the company. This book was to serve as a "road map" for the company's next generation of leaders so that they could continue to achieve enduring business success.

Five years later, this book has morphed into something more than "just another business book," because it also includes Peter's personal stories of failure, overcoming obstacles, successes and navigating changes in life that show how the principles that apply for success in business apply as readily to the principles for success in life.

This book is written from my point of view as I interview Peter. The writing of this book is also a story within the book.

From Rust to Trust:
Peter's Tips
for Living a Principle-Centered
and Other-Focused Life

Chapter 1

How to Grow a Rubber Tree in Maryland

"The meaning of life is to find your gift; the purpose of life is to give it away."
~ Pablo Picasso ~

"How are you feeling about your race on Sunday?" I asked Peter over the phone.

It was Friday night and Peter was racing in the Ironman Triathlon® on Sunday. More than 2,500 athletes including Peter would attempt to finish the triathlon with its 2.4 mile swim, 112-mile bike ride and 26.2-mile run in their quest to achieve the finish line and hear these magical words: "You are an Ironman®!" As Peter's triathlon coach, I was curious about how ready he felt for the race and whether or not he needed a pep talk to boost his confidence.

"I feel good," answered Peter. "I feel like I've already won it."

I didn't understand, so I asked, "What do you mean?"

"Well, racing on Sunday is like growing a rubber tree in Maryland," he said. "Can a rubber tree survive in Baltimore, Maryland? Normally, no, because the conditions aren't right; there isn't enough rain and the climate in winter is too harsh, too cold and too difficult. Growing a rubber tree in Maryland is not easy; however, with good roots, the right soil and lots of attention, it can. The rubber tree will overcome adversity and harsh conditions to prosper and live on for an eternity."

I knew rubber trees didn't typically grow in Maryland, but I liked the metaphor.

Peter continued, "My Ironman race is like growing a rubber tree. Preparing for the race has been a rocky journey for me this year that started with an injury. Work commitments and frequent travel impacted my training. Yet, here I am about to start the race. As my coach, you're part of my team along with my wife, Kathy; my daughter, Katie; my swim coach, John; my Pilates instructor; my personal trainer; my massage therapist and everyone else. I am like a rubber tree in Baltimore, getting lots of attention from a team of people who care about me so that I can finish the race on Sunday in spite of the adversity that led up to it."

I reflected back on my own experiences as a triathlete. Because of the amount of time and commitment it takes to train for three different sports, successfully preparing for an Ironman requires a big support team. As a triathlete I had spent thousands of dollars on massage therapists, chiropractors and yoga instructors over the years.

"The rubber tree metaphor applies to business, too," he added. "My company, Mid-Atlantic Rubber, manufactures and distributes rubber parts for other companies that make anything from refrigerators to motorcycles. Parts range from rubber gaskets to shock mounts. Following a record year in 2008, our sales were down more than 35% in 2009 driven by the economic recession, yet Mid-Atlantic bounced back in 2010 and achieved record profits in spite of being in a primarily commodity driven industry competing on the basis of price amidst an ailing, fear-driven economy. When you bring a team of people together with the same purpose and create a high trust culture, a business can survive in adverse conditions, just like a rubber tree can grow in adverse conditions. My coaching business had been effected by the economic recession, too.

I listened thoughtfully as Peter continued."

"My rubber tree journey has been exceptional for me professionally as a business owner and as a triathlete. I want to help others go from rust to trust and get to their own finish line by encouraging them to take that first step at the start line and then have the attitude and strength to persevere. Maybe they are trying to quit smoking, trying to lose weight, or trying to change careers. They could be buying a house, being a caregiver, or battling a health issue—it really doesn't matter—it's their Ironman. Their eventual success will inspire countless others who are close to them to also take that first step, to begin their journey from rust to trust."

"So what is the first step to go from rust to trust?" I asked Peter.

Chapter 2
I Meet Peter

"The will to win, the desire to succeed, the urge to reach your full potential...these are the keys that will unlock the door to personal excellence."
~ Confucius ~

I first met Peter in 2009 when he was looking for ways to become a faster triathlete. A triathlete friend had suggested to Peter that he do a VO_2max test, an exercise test performed on a treadmill or stationary bicycle that measures how much oxygen his body uses while exercising at increasing levels of intensity. The test results would show Peter's potential as an endurance athlete, in other words, his maximal oxygen uptake. The exercise physiologist performing the test would also be able to provide guidelines to Peter on how to train more effectively using his heart rate monitor and rate of perceived effort.

Peter was referred to Krista, a local exercise physiologist in Baltimore who coached triathletes, runners and cyclists. One of Krista's specialties was VO_2max testing.

The first thing Peter remembered noticing when he entered Krista's office was her trophy and finisher's certificate from the inaugurual Ironman China. Krista had completed the inaugural event the previous year on a small island off the coast of mainland China. She had finished third in her age group and won a very unique trophy.

When I later asked him about the trophy, Peter replied, "Part of it was that I had recently lived in Singapore and the other part was that I was getting ready for Ironman Lake Placid in New York. Krista told me her story that she decided to do this race with her coaching client even though she was not in total Ironman racing shape."

After Peter filled out a health questionnaire and signed a waiver, Krista had him sit on a stationary bike wearing a plastic mask with tubes that connected the mask to a box, which was connected to a computer to analyze the amount of oxygen he was using while riding.

After Peter did a twenty-minute warm-up on the bike, Krista incrementally increased the resistance of the bike's flywheel, requiring Peter to pedal harder and harder to maintain the same cadence or pedal revolutions per minute. After a few minutes Peter said he was 'pedaling for his life' and then quickly reached exhaustion. Peter later told me that he was so inspired by Krista's race in China that he asked her if she would coach him for Ironman Triathlon Lake Placid in July. Krista apologized, telling him that she was unable to take on any additional coaching clients at the time but her boyfriend, me, who lived nearby in Virginia was a triathlon coach who specialized in training athletes for Ironman triathlons.

Krista told me briefly about Peter over the phone, "I tested an Ironman athlete today, Peter O'Dunne, who is looking for a triathlon coach. Are you interested in coaching him? I think he would be a good client."

"Sure, I'll talk to him," I said.

After speaking briefly with Peter on the phone, I agreed to coach him. I mailed him a copy of my book, *Full-Time and Sub Nine: Fitting Iron Distance Training into Everyday Life*. I also emailed him my coaching questionnaire, which he promptly filled out and emailed back to me along with two pictures of himself racing at Ironman Lake Placid the previous year. None of my other clients had ever sent me pictures of themselves before I started coaching them. Peter was already different.

From his questionnaire, I learned that Peter had been a runner before becoming a triathlete. He had worked his way up to marathons and qualified for the Boston Marathon in 1996. He had started triathlons as an alternative to running because he was a pretty good swimmer and thought it might be fun to try a triathlon.

When I later asked Peter what he thought about my book, he said, "I can remember the day that I received your book in the mail. I was so excited to read it when I found out that you were a cancer survivor. I was so impressed with the humility of how you handled the subject. So from the beginning, I looked at you not just as a coach but also as an author."

Our coaching relationship took an upgrade when I decided to move to Towson, Maryland about 15 miles from Peter's house to live with Krista in the fall of 2009. Peter and I began meeting face to face each week to workout and then grab coffee afterwards.

In October, Peter invited me to join him on his business trip to Boulder, CO so we could swim, bike and run together. Peter had previously traveled to Boulder for a week so he knew where we could swim outdoors, bike up seemingly endless hills and run all over town on the city's trail system. To Peter's amazement, I accepted his invitation and we spent a memorable sixty-four hours together.

We also began talking about writing this book.

Chapter 3

Start with a Vision

"All men dream: but not equally. Those who dream by night in the dusty recesses of their minds wake in the day to find that it was vanity: but the dreamers of the day are dangerous men, for they may act their dream with open eyes, to make it possible."
~ *T.E. Lawrence, Seven Pillars of Wisdom, 1926* ~

Peter and I faced each other across a small table over coffee one Tuesday morning. We had met early at the fitness center, swam laps and lifted weights before heading over to the coffee shop to begin discussing the stories for this book. This would become our routine for many months.

"How did Mid-Atlantic thrive through the economic recession in 2008?" I began.

Peter replied, "Let me go back more than twenty five years to before I worked for Mid-Atlantic. I was working at another company, Data General, at the time, but I had a dream to own my own company one day. My vision was to be a business owner and to treat employees the way I wanted to be treated."

Peter then told me the story of how he first met Clarence, the owner of Mid-Atlantic Rubber Company at a tradeshow. After the trade show, Peter handwrote Clarence a letter to thank Clarence for his time and tell him how much he appreciated talking to him. Peter handwrote the letter because he wanted to connect with Clarence differently and more personally by doing something that most people didn't do.

Peter didn't hear from Clarence about Mid-Atlantic until five years later when Kathy and he were living in Singapore and both working for Data General.

"Clarence called me in Singapore and asked me to come to Baltimore to help him manage Mid-Atlantic and eventually take over the company," said Peter.

"You must have really made an impression with your letter," I commented.

He nodded. "It's often the small, simple things that do make the difference. I also had a clear vision of my future. I wanted to do something special— my metaphor of growing a rubber tree in Maryland from the ground up. I wanted to plant and grow a rubber tree that would prosper through the cold winters and hot summers of Maryland or, in business terms, a business that would successfully survive economic downturns and fickle customers and thrive in all conditions. That was my vision."

Peter handed me a piece of paper with Mid-Atlantic's vision statement:

Together, Mid-Atlantic Rubber Company will dramatically impact the lives of our employees and their families.

Peter explained how the Mid-Atlantic management team had developed several drafts and presented them to the company employees to discuss and edit before coming up with the final version.

Peter added, "Mid-Atlantic's vision was based on my original vision to treat others as I would like to be treated. I think that's where visions come from—deep inside of leaders."

He continued, "I also have a vision of myself as a triathlete to compete in the Ironman World Championship in Kona, Hawaii one day. Almost anyone can do a triathlon if they really want to do it and are willing to do the training, but only a few will work hard enough and smart enough to earn the right to compete in the World Championship. "Competing at Kona is the exception rather than the norm." I commented.

"Yes," he said, "it's simply not enough to begin training; you also have to commit, develop a plan, learn, train smartly, set goals, work hard for an extended period of time, and surround yourself with a good support team—just like successfully running a business."

From my own experiences I knew that vision statements were meant to be aspirational in nature and to serve as a guide to decision-making. Being a self-employed business owner, I was doing a multitude of things as an athlete, a triathlon coach, a race director and a writer. I asked Peter what he recommended that someone like me should do in order to come up with a vision statement.

Peter answered, "Choose a vision which originates from something you are passionate about. Sadly, not very many people are truly doing something that they are passionate about. Take the time to reflect. What gets you excited to wake up in the morning? If money didn't make any difference, what would you like to be doing? Identify the perfect job that solves a problem or fulfills a need. Try volunteering—read to people, teach or coach kids for the Special Olympics. Write down all your thoughts and look for common themes."

"That sounds easy enough," I said.

"It may actually be harder than you think to come up with your own unique vision for you," replied Peter. "Creating a vision can be a frustrating and iterative process. Begin by writing something down and then sit with it for a while. Ask others for input with the understanding that only you can truly define your vision. But remember your vision is simply the starting point. Once you have a vision, the fun starts as you begin to transfer the vision from an idea on paper to a result or accomplishment."

Chapter 4

Taking a First Step with Courage and Faith

"Faith is taking the first step even when you don't see the whole staircase."
~ Martin Luther King, Jr. ~

Our coffee shop meetings had become routine. We usually sat in the same spot if the table was available. We both ordered the same drinks every time. If I was hungry, I might also order a bowl of oatmeal.

"You see," began Peter, "having a vision is still only the starting point. You now have to take that first step up a dark staircase when you can't see where it leads. That first step requires courage and faith; courage to take the risk and do something with uncertainty and faith to believe everything will ultimately work out. I think that's exactly what courage is: the choice to confront uncertainty."

I asked Peter for an example of courage.

He replied, "My friend and running coach was riding her bike in Baltimore when a driver T-boned her, causing extensive injuries to her legs, shoulder, back, neck and head. She is very fortunate to be alive. Over the past three years, she has had multiple surgeries but still has lingering issues with her back, neck and head. Last year, she was referred to a physician in Dallas who specializes in concussions and neurological damage. Her new treatments, which began almost immediately, included using a hyperbaric chamber, removing scar tissue and laser therapy. She has since progressed to a Dallas physician specializing in retraining the brain and nervous system. It could take up to 200 treatments and lots of visits to Dallas from Baltimore before she is fully cured, if she is ever cured. Besides the uncertainty of getting her health back, there is the issue of paying for all the treatments. Her life may be on hold now, but her courage and positive attitude is alive and very inspiring to all that know her."

"She sounds like an amazing person," I said. "How about a personal example of when you chose to confront uncertainty?"

Peter replied, "Leaving our jobs in Singapore and moving to Baltimore, all on a verbal promise and handshake from Clarence that I would eventually be able to take over Mid-Atlantic Rubber, took a gigantic leap of faith. Kathy and I absolutely loved Singapore and traveling throughout Asia, but Kathy hated her job and our two-year contract at Data General was coming up for renewal. The timing for moving back was perfect because Kathy was pregnant with Katie, who was our primary consideration. We really looked forward to buying a house and settling down after five years of traveling together as a married couple."

He continued, "So Kathy and I came up with our Baby in the Oven Plan or 'BITOP.' I would work for Mid-Atlantic and Kathy would stop working in order to take care of Katie and all of our household matters. My first step up the dark stairway towards my vision of owning my own company was leaving our jobs and moving to Maryland."

"That sounds risky," I commented.

Peter nodded and said, "Yes I was taking a job with a company that I had not even visited and had no benefits. We were going from two incomes to one. We were flying blind and had no safety net. I remember thinking how important it was to believe in myself and my ability to make it work.

Success happens for lots of reasons, but I think one of the keys is not having a safety net to fall back on."

I asked him what it was like after they moved to Baltimore.

"The first few weeks were exciting but it become old," he replied. "We missed being settled with our stuff. We were uncertain about where we would be living and uncertain about the job plus there was the pressure of Kathy being pregnant. Our life had suddenly been turned upside down. Everything that was certain in our lives was now uncertain.

"We wondered if we had made a mistake in moving back to Maryland. You might think it might be weather-related since it was wintertime and we had just been in Singapore for two years. But it wasn't the weather. The biggest obstacles were at work. Two key Mid-Atlantic employees who had been there for a long time did not want me to be there. When Clarence hired me, he did not give me the authority to manage them. I had to lead without authority and without an office for the first year. Getting the business computerized and physically cleaned up required new behaviors, new procedures and processes and frankly new attitudes. Change was something badly needed but was not easily accepted. In short, Mid-Atlantic was pretty rusty."

He continued: "But Clarence was totally supportive of everything I was doing and, little by little, the path to my vision began to materialize. If you think about it, hiring me to eventually take over Mid-Atlantic also took a leap of faith by Clarence. He believed in me enough to offer me the job, train me and then eventually let me run his company in my own way."

"Talk about uncertainty," I said. "Clarence hired you to take over his company after only meeting with you a few times."

Peter nodded and said: "For you, writing this book with me takes faith. It takes lots of faith and courage to take that first step with this book with an uncertain outcome and a significant time commitment that takes away from the other things that you're doing."

I replied, "I hadn't really thought about the book like that, but you're right. I do have doubts and uncertainty about what the outcome of the book will be. Will people read it? Will it open more doors for me as an author? I don't know."

Peter smiled. "Taking that first step with uncertainty is something that most people don't do because it's uncomfortable and it takes courage. It takes incredible courage to embrace change. Who would ever think of a triathlon coach as a writer? It really is a huge 'win-win' for both of us. You get to do something you love, writing, and then you can use this book to build your portfolio of books with this one always being your best and most favorite! For me, my company and I get the opportunity to capture our history, legacy, principles and culture in stories for future generations. I'm also creating a learning tool to help other people and businesses."

"What about courage in triathlons?" I asked.

He replied, "When I think of courage, I think of all those triathletes who are starting in an open water swim for the first time with 2,000 other triathletes treading water next to them waiting for the starting gun and the mass chaos of churning arms and legs that follows."

"Yes," I answered. "In my experiences as a coach, many triathletes have a fear of the open water. A few years ago, I had a client training for an Ironman who cried before she entered the water for a practice open water swim with only a few other triathletes present. I remember talking with her through the experience and encouraging her to swim in spite of her fear."

Peter nodded. "Courage takes shape in many ways."

"What amazed me," I continued, "was that she was able to overcome her fear and completed her Ironman swim successfully two months later. How about you? When did you take the first step towards achieving your vision to compete in the Ironman World Championship?"

He smiled. "I've had the dream of competing in Kona for a long time, but it wasn't until I met my friend Jonathan in 2001 that I began taking steps towards accomplishing that goal. Jonathan was a lifeguard at the fitness center where I worked out, and he had just won the Atlantic City Marathon. I remember thinking, 'Wow! This guy is an incredible athlete!' so of course I wanted to meet and talk to him."

"I walked up to Jonathan, introduced myself and congratulated him on his victory. I learned that he was training for the Ironman in Lake Placid,

New York. Then he told me that I could do one, too. By believing in me, he helped me to have faith in myself to take that first step forward by signing up for my first Ironman Lake Placid in 2005 after several years racing shorter distance triathlons. Jonathan even coached me for that first Ironman race and helped me buy a real triathlon bike."

"You're lucky you met Jonathan," I said.

"Yes," answered Peter. "Jonathan had been a financial analyst but became disenchanted with the company because he saw people violating principles all the time. So he left and decided to become a professional triathlete. He had joined the fitness center as a lifeguard so that he could train for triathlons full time."

I asked, "So Jonathan's goal to be a professional triathlete and the resulting actions that he took inspired you to find the courage to take that first step towards your goal?"

"Yes," said Peter. "Just as Clarence believed in my ability to lead and grow Mid-Atlantic, Jonathan believed in me for my first Ironman. I hope that we can inspire someone else to make their first step after they read this book."

Chapter 5

What Is Your Purpose?

"I can't die; it would ruin my image."
~ Jack LaLanne, fitness legend and motivational speaker who finally died at age 96 ~

"One day," Peter said to me over coffees, "You will be in a room and realize you are the most powerful person in the room. What will you do? Will you leverage the situation for your own benefit or will you try to leverage the situation for the benefit of others?"

I thought for a second then answered, "I would hope that I would try to help others."

"Why would you do that?" replied Peter. "You have the most power. You could do whatever you want. No one could stop you."

"True, but I wouldn't feel good about myself," I said.

"Why is that?" he asked.

I thought for a second. "Because it's not who I am. It's not what I'm about."

"Ah," said Peter. "So what you are telling me is that taking advantage of others for your own selfish gain does not align with your personal mission statement—your statement of what you're all about."

"What do you mean by my personal mission statement?" I asked him.

"Based on your answer to my question about being the most powerful person in the room," he answered, "I think you already have a personal mission statement—or at least an idea of what you're all about—even if your mission statement is not formally written down."

Peter went on to explain how a personal mission statement is very much like a company mission statement. As CEO, he helped write Mid-Atlantic's mission statement with input from the employees. Peter had printed out a copy of Mid-Atlantic's mission statement and handed it to me:

To grow profitably by caring for our employees as owners, our customers as guests, and our suppliers as partners, in a prevention environment with focus and interdependence. Together, we will discover new applications for sealing, protecting, and connecting Mid-Atlantic Rubber with global industry.

Peter then said, "I believe people have unlimited potential, but they need purpose and a way to contribute, which is what the mission statement spells out for them. If you read through it, you'll see that we care not only about our customers who we're selling to, but we also care about our employees—we want to treat them like owners—and we care about our suppliers as partners. Because we involved our employees in the creation of the mission statement, they also have an ownership stake in it."

"Okay, I get it," I said. "Mid-Atlantic's mission states that the company wants to grow profitability and profitability enables the business to continue to provide jobs for employees, buy from suppliers and sell products and services to customers."

"Exactly," responded Peter. "The embedded statement that we do this *in a prevention environment with focus and interdependence* gets to how we are going to achieve our business. Prevention, focus and interdependence are three of our core principles. We'll talk about principles another time."

I said, "I notice that Mid-Atlantic has a motto below its mission statement. Can you talk about that?"

Peter replied, "Our motto is *'Solutions that seal and protect by people who care and connect.'* It means that we protect our customers by making their problems and their concerns ours. Caring is a process of finding and removing pain. It applies to all our relationships. People that do care, connect. Connecting creates relationships and loyalty for customers, suppliers, and employees."

"The key, though," he continued, "is that it's not enough to have a mission, motto and vision statement, but they must be integrated into the business or, in the case of a personal mission statement, integrated into your life."

"How do you do that?" I asked. "I mean, I've worked at a number of companies in the past and each company had mission statements, but I wouldn't say the mission statements were truly integrated into the business. They were sometimes posted on the wall and published in annual reports, but otherwise mission statements didn't affect me in my day to day work."

"So, yes, we post our mission statement on the wall, too," replied Peter, "but we also try to live it every day. We talk about our company mission during our weekly team meetings and our quarterly company meetings. Our management team constantly reinforces the mission with our employees. Rather than just being a sign on the wall, we use our mission statement to guide our company's actions. We keep it alive."

He continued, "We also go another step deeper at Mid-Atlantic in that each of our three teams—Sales, Cash-Flow and Warehouse—has its own team mission statement, which provide a purpose for each team and describes how each team member contributes to the team goals."

"Can you give me an example of how a team mission statement applies to one of your employees in their day to day work?" I asked him.

"Sure," said Peter. "As stated in Mid-Atlantic mission, we strive to treat our employees like owners and our suppliers like partners. One of our employees is in charge of purchasing. She has developed very good relationships with our suppliers that extend beyond business-to-business transactions. She knows and asks about their families, which demonstrates that she cares about them as partners, not just business transactions. As an employee, when her husband had surgery, her manager let her take off a week without using sick or vacation time. She missed a whole week of work but her manager let her work from home where she could call into meetings."

"Those are great examples," I responded. "Earlier when you asked me what I would do if I was the most powerful person in the room and whether I would take advantage of other people or not, I said 'No.' You then said that was an example of living my own mission statement."

"Yes," said Peter. He then shared his personal mission statement:

To inspire "greatness" in myself and others by LOVING, LEARNING, LEADING, and LIVING in a "Godly" and "Christ-like" manner.

Peter explained, "I discovered a long time ago that I feel best when I am helping others. I am an optimist and extremely positive. When I combine those gifts with being other-focused, it helps me see the best in others. So for me, my purpose is to inspire others and myself towards greatness. Towards being or doing the very best. My key principles are: Leadership, Love, Living life, and Learning. I am a Christian and believe that Christ was the greatest role model and leader ever. I like the expression WWJD (What would Jesus do?). Having this reference as part of my personal mission keeps me grounded and reminds that I have been put here on earth with my uniqueness to serve God and others. Purpose and contribution are what get me out of bed in the morning."

"How does someone go about creating a personal mission statement?" I asked.

"Become aware of your feelings and write something down," stated Peter, "Putting thoughts on paper is the first step to integrating your personal mission into your life. It eventually becomes more than a thought or an idea but rather a tangible object that you can figuratively stick in your back pocket as a reminder of what you're all about. If you stick with it, you will detect your life's mission."

"How important is it to have a mission statement?" I asked.

He answered, "My experience when riding my bike seems to be that, without fail, whenever I take my eye off the road, or start daydreaming, I find myself nearly missing (and sometimes hitting) a pothole or road debris. The parallels in life and business are numerous. Focusing on what's important is the key, whether it's growing profits 10% annually in a business, crossing the finish line in a triathlon or graduating from college. When you don't have the right focus or lose focus, all kinds of potholes appear."

He added "For me, my mission statement helps me by providing focus to reduce the number of potholes in life, and, if I do hit a pothole, I can recover quickly to get back on track. Potholes and setbacks are not all bad, as they keep me humble and force me to continually improve. They also remind me that things are never perfect and that so many things are outside of my control like tick bites and rain."

Chapter 6

Setting a Foundation with Principles

"Our principles are the springs of our actions. Our actions, the springs of our happiness
or misery. Too much care, therefore, cannot be taken in forming our principles."
~ Red Skelton ~

By now, the employees at the coffee shop knew our drink orders. I began
our session by asking Peter, "We've talked about having a vision and a mission statement and the analogy of taking the first step up a dark stairway.
What happens if the stairway ends or it splits and you have to choose a
new direction? How do you know then what's the best choice to make?"

"That's a great question," replied Peter, "and the answer is surprisingly simple. You may not always know what the best choice will ultimately be, but
the key to making better decisions is using sound principles. Principles
are the unwritten laws that govern us. Our principles are the lens through
which we make our decisions. Think of them as the roots or the foundation
upon which everything about you is built."

"Can you give me an example?" I asked.

"Sure, David. Principles govern how a farmer grows corn. A farmer can't sit on his butt all spring and summer then plant seeds in July and expect a full harvest in September. Successful farming is a year around effort that requires principles like: planning, timing, hard work, dedication and decision-making. There are no shortcuts in farming to long-term success."

Peter then explained how Mid-Atlantic explicitly defines three core principles in its mission statement: prevention, focus and interdependence. These three principles describe the culture that he was trying to develop.

When I asked him for an example, Peter said, "Interdependence involves a trusting relationship where both parties are truly interested in helping each other to win. At Mid-Atlantic we cross train our employees to work in other areas so we can move them around where we need them to be. Let's say for example that our customers are waiting for parts and we have an order from our suppliers coming in next Thursday. When the order is delivered to our warehouse, all of our employees pitch in to get the parts shipped out as soon as possible. It does not matter who you are in the organization. Warehouse employees might get pulled from die cutting to sort parts. Sales employees might help with receiving truck shipments and putting parts away."

When I asked him what's unique about Mid-Atlantic, he answered, "We always choose to do the right thing for the customer regardless of whose fault it may be or what the expense might be. For example, when one of our parts suppliers increased their prices on us after an order had already been placed, we chose to pay the extra expenses rather than pass them on to our customers. We wouldn't dream of increasing an order cost to a customer after the order had been placed."

"Did your relationship change with the parts vendor after their actions?" I asked.

"Yes, we lost our ability to trust them," he said. "Was it worth it for them? In the short term they made more money, but they damaged our relationship, which hurt them in the long run."

Peter continued, "Principles also apply when training for a triathlon. Being successful in triathlon requires principles like hard work, dedication and decision-making."

"I agree," I replied. "Unfortunately, I see many triathletes looking for short-cuts in training. In our sport, a short cut might be doing excessive amounts of higher intensity training without developing an endurance base, which builds fitness quickly but also leads to a greater chance of burnout, injury or both. Another short cut is cheating. There are race officials at triathlons to enforce the rules, but they can't be everywhere at once so it's really up to each individual athlete to decide if they want to cheat or not as there is only a small risk of receiving a penalty."

"Absolutely," said Peter. "Those are examples of not following sound principles. If faced with a decision on whether or not to use an illegal performance enhancing drug, the principle of honesty is a powerful deterrent to cheating."

"When we are grounded in principles," he continued, "we have purpose in life. Without principles, we invite disaster. Without principles, it's easy to follow someone else's agenda and do what 'everyone else' is doing. It's like giving the remote control to your life to someone else to use. Having grounded principles make the harder decisions easier to make by providing boundaries or parameters within which to decide. When decisions are tough, you can fall back on your principles to make better choices. Principles are the pathway from rust to trust."

Chapter 7

Stumbling Blocks

"There is no such thing as a problem without a gift for you in its hands.
You seek problems because you need their gifts."
~ Richard Bach, author of Jonathan Livingston Seagull ~

Peter's goal to race at the Ironman in Hawaii continued to be elusive. With this year's racing season over and the holiday season beginning, Peter traveled more in order to visit customers and he trained less. He indulged in more food and alcohol, gaining nearly twenty pounds in a few months. The extra weight slowed him down and I could tell it affected his self-image when I talked to him.

He reflected back, "It was fun not being regimented to a training schedule and diet. However, weeks later the bad habits had found their way to my hips and belly and I was forced to make a change. I did not like what I saw in the mirror. There are always consequences for violating principles. When the pain gets great enough, people will change. That's what happened to me."

During this time, Peter would often call me and leave me messages like: "Hey, David, this is Peter. I'm just calling to let you know that I'm thinking of you and wish we could be outside doing a bike ride together. The weather here is so nice. Let me know if I can do anything for you."

After I listened to his messages, I always felt better.

Peter admitted that his food vice is Cheez-Its, especially when he drives for long periods of time. He'll sometimes eat an entire box in one sitting— that's more than 1,200 calories and more than half of what his caloric intake should be for the entire day.

"Why the entire box?" I asked him over the phone.

"Stress and availability," Peter answered. I think the Cheez-Its also had to do with drinking wine. No wine, no Cheez-Its. Drinking wine was a way to deal with the stress."

"I get that," I answered. "My food vices are dark chocolate and cheese. If I keep either of these things in the house, then I'm prone to eat the entire chocolate bar or half the block of cheese. But, if the chocolate and cheese are not in the house, I don't eat them because they are inconvenient. I find another snack instead that is more readily available like an apple or a handful of almonds."

At my request, Peter began to record his food intake and calories in a nutrition log online so that we could both monitor his food choices. He began to eat better.

Peter called me early one morning and left me a voicemail to let me know he had hurt his hamstring while training at the gym. He had felt something 'snap' while sprinting indoors but didn't elaborate in his message. I called him back to ask about the injury and left a message.

I received his email later that night:

> Hello David. Thanks for your call tonight. You always know the right things to say. My gut tells me that my injury will last more than 2

weeks. I will know Tuesday when I see you. We might have to completely refocus my training but the end in mind is still the same with the injury being a bump in the road. I have been standing more than I should be. My hamstring doesn't bother me unless I try to run across the street—which I can't do at all.

Thanks for thinking of me. See you Tuesday. Peter

Peter had an MRI done and saw his physical therapist who subsequently emailed me after seeing him:

Peter's MRI report does not sound good. It's definitely a significant tear. The challenge for athletes is to listen to their bodies. Peter said he started to feel this hamstring during the workout, but kept pushing himself anyway. The hamstring tore because it was already slightly injured and couldn't take the added load of the high intensity speed work.

Frank and honest communication is the key, especially on the part of the athlete. Peter may not have expressed that he was still feeling some hamstring pain from his last triathlon to his trainer—thus the trainer didn't know to adjust the workout appropriately. As athletes we tend to hide things sometimes in an effort to keep pushing—thinking our bodies can handle it. It's the 'what doesn't kill us makes us stronger' mentality.

It's a lesson learned the hard way and never forgotten. Peter seems to have a good attitude about it and does not blame anyone except himself for the injury.

I now had a coaching client with a torn hamstring who couldn't run. Yet, Peter in his normal, cheerful way, accepted the injury and didn't complain even though I could tell he was upset about it.

When we met on Tuesday, I asked Peter about his hamstring injury.

Although unable to run, he said that he was feeling better then said, "Stumbling blocks like injuries in athletics can also easily happen with relationships when secrets are kept or when there is a departure from principles like honesty and transparency. I had two such stumbling blocks involving money and the Mid-Atlantic building. Kathy's father had really encouraged me to buy the building that Mid-Atlantic was renting and offered to loan me the down payment by cashing in some of his CDs that were coming up for renewal. I offered him a much better interest rate than he was currently able to get and our agreement was made."

"Sounds like a 'win-win,'" I said.

He shook his head in the negative. "It would have been, but the problem was that I never discussed this with Kathy to ask for her approval. Maybe I never asked her so she wouldn't worry or maybe because I knew she would say, "No." Of course she found out later and was understandably upset. She also shared with me that she never, ever wanted to borrow money from her parents. Kathy and I immediately got a loan and paid her father back."

He continued, "Eight years later, I stumbled again by taking out a sizable second mortgage on the Mid-Atlantic building, without telling Kathy, in order to fund the purchase of ice machines from Italy for a friend of mine in the foodservice business. The machines did not sell and I was on the hook for a sizable loss. I opened the wound from my previous mistake all over again. That's how they cane people in Singapore. A sentencing of six strokes of the cane might be spread out over Three years. Each year the person caning opens up the same wounds from the caning the year before. How could I have done this again? Was it because I did not want to worry Kathy or because I knew she would say no? It takes some people longer to 'get it,' but I finally did. Kathy and I are partners and we need to make decisions together, especially really important decisions. I learned a lot from those two stumbling blocks. Kathy is usually right, and I value her as my partner. Following my personal principles like honesty and open communication has kept me from making more mistakes like this, but it took a while to regain my trust with Kathy."

I said, "We've talked about some stumbling blocks, whether they are injuries, bad decisions or bad circumstances. You've also said that having a written, detailed vision and mission statement helps you manage through the potholes and bumps along the way to goals. How do you tie in principles?"

He answered, "It's the same with principles. We use principles like 'honesty' and 'listening to our bodies' to help guide decisions and choices. There will be obstacles. The best thing we can do is navigate the obstacles as best as we can by holding our vision close, following our mission statement and using our principles to make decisions. In my experience, most of my obstacles, which could be seen as problems, offered me a moment of clarity and an opportunity for me to make a change."

Chapter 8

Culture

"Yesterday I was clever, so I wanted to change the world.
Today I am wise, so I am changing myself."
~ Rumi, 13th-century Persian poet ~

In July 2010, I followed Krista, my soon to be fiancé, to Boulder. She had received a job offer and I was eager to move west, especially to Boulder with its active, healthy lifestyle. Although the move prevented me from being able to meet with Peter in person as much, my move to Boulder gave Peter another reason to visit Boulder when he met with one of his customers in Colorado.

When Peter came to visit a few months after my move, he began our conversation by discussing Mid-Atlantic Rubber. "Every team, every family, every business and every country has a culture, a set of shared behaviors and beliefs. Today, our culture at Mid-Atlantic is such that everyone is considered a valuable asset to the business and we care about each other.

This is not just lip service; caring is really there. For example, our management team makes it a point to know the families of individual employees. If an employee needs help with money, moving or time off, we try to help him or her if we can. At work, we've set up an exercise room and a serenity room for employees to take breaks. We give out bonuses and try to 'share the wealth' as much as possible. We even have a Slurpee machine in the summer."

"Those are some nice perks," I said.

Peter continued, "Trust is also a big part of our culture. We share company financials and forecasts through weekly and quarterly meetings with all of our employees. We have open, two-way communication between management and employees. We're straight up and don't hide anything. There are no time clocks at Mid-Atlantic. Every employee has his own timesheet, totals up his own hours at the end of week and turns it in. Ultimately, we're building a bond and relationship with our employees. The end result is that we have employees who are dedicated and work for us for many years."

I nodded and said, "What struck me as odd was that every Mid-Atlantic employee I talked to said the same thing: 'I like coming to work.' How rare that must be."

Peter replied, "The bottom line is that Mid-Atlantic as a company has to achieve results. We value the uniqueness of our employees, customers, suppliers, as it creates a culture of synergy and abundance. We make sure to take the time to hire people who fit with our culture and get rid of those who later prove that they don't fit. We want to thrive; we do not want to become a 'me, too' business that does the same thing as every other business does. That's the way to become rusty, obsolete and extinct."

He continued, "I remember my trip to Scotland with Katie's youth group when she was fifteen years old. We spent a lot of time on a bus traveling from city to city and hotel to hotel. I was anxious to find an Internet connection to catch up with things back home, but the hotels where we were staying did not have quality Internet service. As we approached our hotel on the fifth evening of the trip, I remember laughing not only at the name of the hotel—'The Honest Lawyer Hotel'—but at the poor condition of the building. The roof was covered in moss. For sure, I thought, an Internet connection won't exist in this dumpy hotel. I was wrong. The Honest Lawyer turned out to be the nicest hotel with the best Internet and the best food of our trip. From that point on, I'd always say, 'You can't always tell the quality of the hotel by the moss on its roof.' It's true of buildings, businesses and people. The culture in a business and the character in a person are both on the inside."

"That's a great example," I said.

"Cities have their own culture, too," said Peter, "You live in Boulder, which has a culture of fitness and health."

"True," I replied. "There are a lot of active people here. On the weekends, there are so many cyclists on the roads and runners on the trails that you would think there is a race going on rather than just the locals doing their rides and runs. Every restaurant has gluten-free options and there are three rock-climbing gyms in a population of 100,000 people. Not everyone wants to live in Boulder, for those that do, it is an environment that supports healthy living."

I paused for a second and added, "Triathlon as a sport has its own culture, too. There are unique terms in triathlon like brick workout, T1 and T2. When dressed casually, triathletes tend to wear triathlon-specific brands of clothing and many male triathletes shave their legs."

Peter said, "As you can imagine, changing a culture can be difficult. It requires changing paradigms; changing the way you think about and see things."

Chapter 9
Change and Changing Paradigms

"Discovery consists not in seeking new lands but in seeing with new eyes."
~ Marcel Proust ~

"Let's talk about changing paradigms," I began asking Peter one afternoon over coffee.

Peter said, "A big paradigm shift for me came about after I attended the *7 Habits of Highly Effective People* training class when it came to Baltimore in 2001."

Peter then explained how the *7 Habits* class developed by Stephen Covey consisted of twenty hours of training over three full-days, combining individual and group exercises, video and class discussion. Each habit builds on the previous habit. The first three habits focus on self-mastery and moving from dependence to independence. The second three focus on developing teamwork, collaboration skills, communication skills and moving from independence to interdependence. The final habit focuses on continuous growth and improvement, embodying all the other habits.

Peter said that *The 7 Habits* class seemed like a great training fit for Mid-Atlantic employees but he wanted to participate by himself first to make sure. During the introduction on day one, the facilitator asked the thirty participants to share a brief overview of their backgrounds and the one thing they wanted to take away from the class. Peter was sitting in the back of the room so he spoke next to last. After the introductions, the facilitator then introduced the habits in detail. Peter remembered thinking, "Wow, I don't practice these habits at all."

Peter then said, "When the facilitator explained the fifth habit, the listening habit of empathetic communication, he said that the biggest violation of the habit is that people listen to reply rather than listen to understand. During the twenty-eight introductions before me, what do you think I was doing?"

"Thinking about what you were going to say," I answered.

"Yes," he said, "I was thinking about what I was going to say instead of listening to the other introductions. Being a really good listener means giving all of your attention to the speaker, and then when it is your turn to talk, being careful not to reply with advice or judgment unless invited. This was a new paradigm for me because it changed how I listen. I am still not perfect with my listening skills, but I have greatly improved since then and I am more aware of my communication."

I need to work on my listening skills.

Peter continued, "I left the *7 Habits* class so excited because this class was exactly what I wanted for each employee and for Mid-Atlantic. When I asked how much it would cost to send all of our employees for the three days of training, I was not prepared for the answer: $25,000. Ouch! But, if I was interested, I could travel to Salt Lake City to train to become a *7 Habits* facilitator for only $5,000. Mid-Atlantic would then own a set of *7 Habits* materials so that we could train employees at any time."

"So you become a facilitator?" I asked.

"Eventually, but my very first thought," he said, "was that there is no way I could ever become a facilitator. I had no teaching background and public speaking is way outside of my comfort zone. I had to make an internal paradigm shift from non-facilitator to facilitator." Peter continued, "The training was a memorable five days and, as is almost always the case, I grew as a result of stepping out of my comfort zone. I facilitated my first two classes to our employees several months later. Half of our employees attended from Wednesday through Friday the other half the following Monday through Wednesday. The first two classes were a little rusty, but we did it, and each employee experienced what had been a life changing experience for me. I remember packing up the class room after 6 days of facilitating these two classes. I was so excited that my vision was complete and successful. It's the same feeling I have when I cross the finish line at Lake Placid. We have since done the class for every new employee. We have invited hundreds of our partners to join us and the class continues to be one of our ongoing leadership development tools. You never know what a difference you can make for yourself and others by changing paradigms and stepping out of your comfort zone."

"What about an example of a paradigm shift at Mid-Atlantic?" I asked.

"We had a very different culture when Bill and I joined Mid-Atlantic more than twenty years ago," Peter replied.

Bill was Mid-Atlantic's General Manager who was first hired part-time in 1990 as a high school senior to work in the afternoons in Mid-Atlantic's co-op program. Bill had interviewed initially with Peter and then with one of the salesmen. Peter said that he quickly hired Bill full time after he graduated because he was principle-centered, worked hard, worked smart, was very trustworthy and showed personal leadership skills from day one. Bill had started with the Warehouse Team handling orders then progressed to Customer Service then Sales then Sales Management until he recently became General Manager.

"The culture was different then for many reasons," Peter continued. "Back then it was an 'us' vs. 'them' mentality meaning it was the 'office people' vs. the 'warehouse people' and the 'sales people' vs. the 'customer,' and so on. The maturity level was very low in the old culture. Attitudes were pessimistic and very negative. The company had a 'no growth' mentality. We were satisfied with only $2 million in sales. All of our employees were contract employees with no benefits. There was no interest or discussion about continuous improvement. If a customer complained or an employee violated a policy, there was no process in place to address the situation. Employees were very resistant to any, and I mean any, type of change. There was no such thing as sharing of information. Information was power. In summary, the culture of the past was all about the 'blame game' and 'victimitis.' It was a culture of rust."

"So, how did the culture change? How did you get from rust to trust?" I asked.

Peter replied, "Change was difficult at first because changing the culture required a change in paradigms—a fundamental change in how management and employees viewed the company and their jobs. The key was to continuously nurture a culture of trust both personally and professionally. I was hands on cleaning the warehouse, packing orders and making improvements to the shipping, receiving, order entry and purchasing process, and especially inventory control and accuracy because these have the biggest impact on the customer. Many times in those early days, we would take an order for parts we showed being in stock, but then we had to call the customer back and likely cancel the order if we could not find the parts. I had to understand and improve the current processes that we were doing manually before we could computerize them. I also wanted employees to see that I cared and that I wanted the workplace to improve."

I commented that the change must have been challenging to the employees.

"It was," said Peter. "and not everyone could adapt. In his role as General Manager, Bill had to fire the sales employee who had interviewed Bill when Bill first joined Mid-Atlantic. Firing the sales employee was not an easy decision since he had been with the company more than twenty-five years. However, the sales employee would not align himself to the company's mission and changed culture. He maintained a sense of entitlement and 'coasting,' as if the rules didn't apply to him—that was Mid-Atlantic's old culture. He learned less and less—he wouldn't even use a computer—and constantly tried to buck the system. Meanwhile, his skill sets became more and more antiquated. The final straw was an action that resulted in a major complaint that could have shut down a major customer's production line."

"That must have been a tough decision for Bill," I said.

"Yes," sighed Peter, "Even though the sales employee had worked for the company for many years, he wasn't willing to change with the changing culture and live within our core principles. Still, Mid-Atlantic remained true to its principle of employee care by paying him a generous severance so that he could re-establish himself somewhere else."

"What is the Mid-Atlantic culture like now?" I asked.

Peter continued, "Today we value and trust everyone at Mid-Atlantic. Continuous improvement is expected. We implement quality assurance practices with processes to track and resolve complaints and mistakes. We also made a fundamental business shift from being a commodity business to customization. Previously, Mid-Atlantic was a catalog parts company with a few forays into specialized parts. Currently, only one-third of our business is catalog parts and the rest is customized parts. Plus, we're moving to application specific products. We now have over $10 million in sales and everyone is an employee with benefits like health care and paid time off."

"What happens when a business doesn't change?" I asked him.

Peter replied, "Not changing can be painful for a business, too. We used to spend $100,000 per year on advertising in the Thomas Register Industrial Directories. For a long time they were the primary form of industrial advertising and the source for all buyers to look for new suppliers. Thomas Register continued to push the paper book version and did not invest in the Internet. They thought that they were too big to fail. As it turned out, they were too expensive not to fail once all their customers realized that there were significantly less expensive options available for advertising. The modern world no longer uses phone books just like the modern business world no longer uses hardback industrial directories. Like Blockbuster Video, Thomas Register eventually moved onto the Internet but only after it was too late."

I added, "A big paradigm change for you was to begin believing you could do an Ironman."

"That's right," he said.

Chapter 10

Getting to Trust

"Few things can help an individual more than to place responsibility
on him, and to let him know that you trust him."
~ *Booker T. Washington* ~

"Why did you choose me to write your book?" I asked Peter.

He replied, "It has always been in the back of my mind to document the Mid-Atlantic Rubber Company story but I was initially thinking about how funny it would be to write a 'play' script. Then I met you and knew that a book was just the right thing. You really helped me by making me answer all those questions before we even started writing, questions about why, who and what. Trust was there from day one."

"I do think the desired end state in a successful culture is both trust and trusting relationships," Peter continued. "Trust is a necessary part of life. We trust doctors to operate on us and to prescribe the correct medicine; we trust pilots to fly the planes and airline employees to de-ice the planes.

Imagine a culture of trust in families, business, churches and governments. Trust does not just happen. Developing trust starts with you. You reap what you sow. Are your own actions trustworthy? It's the concept that you can't help others until you have your own act together."

"How do you know when to trust or not trust someone," I asked.

"People have reputations," Peter said. "The best way for me to develop trust is to really get to know them. Just by spending time together, listening to past stories and discussing how to solve problems or hearing their opinions on things will give you insight to their character. I trust people until they give me a reason or suspicion not to trust them. Still, I am sure you can trust to a fault, especially if it is someone close to you. You may be blinded and not see or hear what you need to see or hear."

"What about trust at Mid-Atlantic?" I asked Peter.

He replied, "Living our principle of interdependence at Mid-Atlantic, involves a trusting relationship where both parties are truly interested in helping each other to win. It means that we cooperate together to accomplish what you want, what I want and what we want together. We cooperate; we become a team and we combine our talents, strengths, abilities and best efforts to achieve our highest success. However, everyone must first move from the dependent level—the attitude of 'you take care of me'—to the independent level—the attitude of 'I am responsible for myself'—before we can reach the interdependence level—the attitude of 'we are responsible together'."

"Can you give me an example?" I asked.

"Sure," he said. "Each week Bill meets with the team leaders and shares the financial forecasts showing how Mid-Atlantic's actual sales are tracking against our goals. When the economic recession hit in 2009, everyone in the company knew that sales were down and that we would have to reduce expenses. We knew that we couldn't support having four full time employees on the Warehouse Team. We had at least a half of a person too many. The easy thing for management to do would have been to fire someone, but we didn't do that."

"Instead," Peter continued, "Bill sat down with all of the members of the

Warehouse Team and told them they had at least half a person too much. He then asked for their input: 'We need to reduce expenses. What do you want us to do?'"

"How did they respond?" I asked.

Peter said, "One of the warehouse employees volunteered to work half time. He demonstrated maturity and initiative by finding a part-time job at another company as a security guard. He has since come back to full-time at Mid-Atlantic once the economy turned around and sales picked back up again."

"Hmmm," I pondered. "Bill was faced with a difficult business decision. Bill communicated the situation to the team affected by the decision and then asked for their input first. The team provided a solution."

"Yes," replied Peter, "Our culture is such that we trust our employees enough to ask for their input. As leaders, we model trustworthiness, as Bill did, by trusting the people in our organization. Ideally, you get the behavior back that you model."

"What happens when an employee breaks trust?" I asked.

Peter said, "I'll give you an example. A few years ago, we had a special die-cutting job that had to be completed by Monday morning so it required working on the weekend to get it done. One of our employees volunteered and we gave him a key to the building. He completed the job, but the productivity logs were inconsistent with his reported hours. Our suspicion prompted us to look at the building security camera, and we discovered that he was working on his car in the front of the building for many of his reported work hours. When we asked him about the productivity report, he would not admit what we already knew was the truth. He could not and would not be honest so we terminated him. But really, he terminated himself. We learned to hire better. We also learned not everyone can work in an unsupervised environment."

"I see the analogies with trust in triathlon," I replied. "In order for our coach-client relationship to be successful, we have to trust each other. You have to trust that I know what I'm doing and that I have your best interests in mind to help you achieve your goals over the long-term. I have to trust that you're doing your workouts and that you're communicating back to me honest feedback. As athletes, we also have to listen to our own bodies and trust what they tell us."

"You've got it," said Peter.

Chapter 11

Leadership Is More Than a Title

"If your actions inspire others to dream more, learn more,
do more and become more, you are a leader."
~ John Quincy Adams ~

Peter and I had talked about the management team at Mid-Atlantic Rubber many times, but he had also said everyone at Mid-Atlantic is a leader.

"Tell me more about leadership," I asked. "What does leadership mean to you?"

"Let me first give you an example of what leadership isn't," Peter replied.

"My sophomore year at Lynchburg College did not start off well. I was not on campus for more than an hour before I found myself in the back of a car heading to a construction site to steal cinder blocks to use for book-cases in my dorm room. Four of us arrived at the construction site around 4 PM, loaded up the car with twelve blocks and headed back to the dorm. A few minutes later, the police pulled us over, found the cinder blocks and arrested us for theft. Apparently, other students had been doing the same thing all day; we just happened to get caught. We spent several hours in jail before we were released on our own recognizance. To make matters worse, the construction site was a Federal post office. We hired a public defender but were found guilty. We appealed and with the help of my father who was an attorney in Baltimore, we were able to have the charge reduced to a misdemeanor. In this story, I was not leading but blindly following."

"I can't imagine you being in jail," I commented.

Peter said, "Back to your original question, David, about what leadership means to me. To me, leadership means to influence other people in a positive way. The hallmark trait of a proactive leader is taking initiative. I like to use the example of a banana peel on the ground. A reactive person might simply step over the banana peel. Others might pick the banana up but look around to make sure someone saw them pick it up. A proactive leader would simply pick it up to prevent an injury to someone else."

Peter continued, "I learned this lesson early in life from my very first boss when I was fifteen. George was the sole proprietor of the Sinclair gas station where I worked every day of high school and on most weekends. Since it was a full service station, there was always a lot to do but there were still moments of no customers. One day, early in my employment, George found me in one of the garage bays leaning against the wall. I will never forget his words to me: 'If you don't have something to do, pick up a broom and go clean the bathrooms.' I don't think the bathrooms had ever been cleaned but by the following week, we had the cleanest bathrooms in all of Baltimore. What George was really teaching me was to be proactive, take initiative, and not wait to be told to do something. If someone has to tell you to do something, it's often too late. At Mid-Atlantic, we want to empower all of our employees, not just the managers, to lead, take initiative and make decisions."

"How about an example in triathlon?" I asked.

"The leadership I witnessed at the 23-mile mark of the run during Ironman Arizona," replied Peter, "was silent, anonymous and worth telling the world. In fact, what I saw was the most memorable part of my Ironman experience that day. I was so impressed by what I saw."

He began, "The story started on Friday night at the athlete dinner and the mandatory pre-race meeting that followed. During the race meeting, the organizers reviewed the rules, the course and the schedule. A different speaker detailed each leg of the race starting with the swim, then the bike and then the run. Within each briefing was also a reminder to the athletes to respect the community, specifically on the bike and run courses, by not littering, and disposing of trash at the aid stations where there were volunteers and trashcans. After all, it was the volunteers who would have to pick up the trash on the course later that night or the next morning."

"Littering on the course in a non-designated area would also result in a time penalty and possible disqualification," I added.

"Fast forward to late in the run," Peter continued. "The Arizona run course is three loops with aid stations every mile. When I reached the start of an aid station, I would stop running and walked through the aid station. I then used the end of the aid station as my starting line to begin running to the next aid station. I became very familiar with the sequence of stuff at the aid stations and learned quickly that the sponges were at the very beginning, followed by the drinks, pretzels and fruit. Finally, there was the 'last chance container' to dispose of trash."

"I had just passed the aid station at mile twenty-three about a quarter-mile back when I came up on a female athlete who was walking. As she was walking, she was bending over to pick up the used sponges littering the ground. She already had several sponges in her hand when I noticed her. 'Wow,' I thought, she is almost a mile to the next aid station and she is picking up dirty, used sponges. She is saving a volunteer from walking a quarter-mile after being on her feet all day long. I can only imagine how many runners saw her and even joined in her effort. I did not think to turn around to get her race number. I am positive that she was picking up the sponges because it was the one thing that she could do to make a difference for someone else in that moment."

"Athletes picking up sponges on the course are definitely not the norm," I commented.

Peter said, "Every post-race awards dinner includes an award for an everyday hero. She was my hero for the day. As leaders do so well, she influenced me, and countless others, without even knowing it by doing something unselfishly for others without recognition. I have told this story to many, many others. All of us can learn and be influenced by that woman's actions. I hope she one day reads this story and smiles."

I said, "Since moving to Boulder, Colorado, I've had the opportunity to meet and train alongside many of the best triathletes and coaches in the world. One of my favorite people in Boulder is six time Ironman World Champion Dave Scott. Even at age sixty, Dave is extremely fit and trains like the champion he is even though he's not racing as much now. What's even more impressive is that Dave has been a coach since he was eighteen years old—so more than forty years now! He knows more about success-fully coaching triathletes than anyone I've ever met. In 2011, he coached Chrissie Wellington and advised Craig Alexander when they both won the Ironman World Championship. Dave is a legend in the sport of the triathlon and arguably the most recognized name in triathlon worldwide. Yet, in spite of all his accomplishments, Dave is humble and willing to poke fun at himself."

"Yes, I know exactly what you mean," Peter replied. "I met Dave at the Luray Triathlon where I had purchased a fundraising opportunity for Katie and I to race the sprint triathlon with him. Katie decided she wanted to do the entire race by herself so it was just Dave and I on the course. At the time, I had a foot injury so was not able to run much. Dave stayed side by side with me the entire race. Even when I was walking on the run, Dave was walking with me. Talk about humility in action."

Peter continued. "There is another element of leadership that Dave Scott demonstrates. Can you guess what that is?"

I shrugged. "No idea."

"Caring," said Peter. "Leaders care about people, like Dave did when he stayed with me during the triathlon."

I smiled. "That's Dave. He's always helping people at his swim and run workouts by providing feedback and making suggestions. There can be more than forty people in the pool swimming laps at his workout, and he will still try to offer individual help to as many people as possible while keeping the lanes moving."

"So, David, let me ask you a question about leadership," said Peter. "Now that you have interviewed numerous leaders in your blog, what would you say is a common characteristic of great leaders?"

I thought for second then said, "Passion is a common characteristic across all the leaders I interviewed," I answered, "Passion is about doing something the best you can for the enjoyment of doing it without the need for external validation or reward. Isn't passion simply another form of caring?"

Peter nodded. "What would the world be like if everyone cared? It feels great as a leader to get results but it feels even better to know that in addition to getting results, you are helping to develop future leaders. That sums up for me the two primary responsibilities of great leaders: getting results and developing the next generation of leaders."

Chapter 12

Goal Setting

"If you don't know where you are going, you will probably end up somewhere else."
~ Lawrence J. Peter ~

"Are you familiar with race walking?" Peter asked me over the phone.

"A little bit," I replied. Peter explained how race walking differs from running in that you must keep one foot on the ground at all times and the front leg must remain straight until it is on the ground and the back leg is lifted.

Peter said, "My father-in-law, Dick, and his wife, Evelyn, like to volunteer so they volunteered at the Senior Olympics in North Carolina one year. When Dick saw the race walking events, he thought they looked like fun so wanted to try them."

He continued, "As Dick prepared for the qualifying race to qualify for the Senior Olympics, he did what he thought at the time was adequate preparation. His time was fast enough to qualify for the Senior Olympics but his performance made him realize that he was not prepared at all for real success. So, Dick created a training program. He set challenging goals each week for himself and each time he achieved a goal, he set the bar a little bit higher. He closely tracked his progress, peaking three days before the race then took the final two days off to rest up for race day."

"What happened on race day?" I asked Peter.

He replied, "The five kilometer race took place on a quarter mile track; it was just over thirteen laps. Dick started out quickly and heard someone yell, 'You'll never keep that pace.' But Dick had a plan; he'd 'burn it up' for the first mile, 'slack off' for the second mile then 'pour it on' again for the last 1.1 miles. Dick later said that he was on a 'mental high' and never slacked off as much as planned, lapping the field to take gold in a personal best time of just over 35 minutes."

"For the 1,500m race later in the day," Peter continued, "Dick competed against the reigning national champion. With little chance for him to capture gold, Dick knew he had a chance at the silver. Just like in the 5,000m event, Dick started out fast and one of his competitors told him that he would never be able to keep it up. On the final lap, the same man pulled even with Dick and said, 'Now, we'll see who has the most left,' and pulled ahead. As they approached the finish line, Dick caught up to his competitor and they crossed the finish line in a photo finish for second place. Their finish times were identical, but Dick took the silver because his foot came down just in front of his competitor's foot. Dick's training plan and preparation paid off, taking him beyond his own expectations with a gold and silver."

'That's awesome," I said.

Peter said, "The reason I'm sharing this story is because we've talked about Mid-Atlantic's mission statement, but we haven't talked about how we actually go about achieving our mission. The 'how' is by setting goals."

I told him about how goal setting reminded me of *Alice and the Cheshire Cat in Alice in Wonderland*:

Alice: *Would you tell me, please, which way I ought to go from here?*

Cheshire Cat: *That depends a good deal on where you want to get to.*

Alice: *I don't much care where.*

Cheshire Cat: *Then it doesn't much matter, which way you go.*

Alice: *...so long as I get SOMEWHERE.*

Cat: *Oh, you're sure to do that, if only you walk long enough.*

I told Peter about my Sports Psychology class where we talked about the benefits of goal setting. In a comprehensive review of studies on goal setting, researchers found that 90% of those who set goals saw positive or partially positive effects, concluding that the beneficial effects of goal setting are some of the most solid and repeatable findings in psychological literature.

"I absolutely believe that," responded Peter. "Every year in January, the Mid-Atlantic management team sets aside two days for annual planning—one day to look backwards and one day to look forwards. We review accomplishments as well as problems and set new initiatives for the coming year. By looking backwards, we can compare how we did against our prior year's goals. As we move forward, we can track against our future goals."

"It's what triathlon coaches call an annual training plan," I said. "An annual training plan is the big picture or road map of an athlete's entire training season."

Peter said, "I remember the first thing that you had me do as your coaching client was to fill out a lengthy questionnaire, which included listing out my past results—looking back—and my goals for the coming season—looking forward—so that we could discuss them both in our initial meeting."

I nodded. "Your annual training plan also served as a guide to help me plan your training for the year to ensure that the workouts I gave you aligned with you and your goals. Whenever I sat down to create your weekly work-out schedule, I referenced your annual training plan as a guideline."

"Similarly at Mid-Atlantic," continued Peter, "we have weekly meetings with each of the teams to review how we've done to date and to talk about how and what we expect to do that week. Each team also has team goals aligned with the larger company goals. We drill down another level so that each employee has individual goals and objectives tied to their individual roles. So not only does the company have goals but each team and each individual within a team have goals that ultimately align with the company's mission statement and culture."

I asked him what happened to Mid-Atlantic's financial goals when the economy tanked unexpectedly a few years ago.

"Good question," replied Peter. "When things changed unexpectedly, we reset our goals and refocused."

"That makes sense," I said. "The same approach applies for triathlon training as well. When you tore your hamstring, we shifted your goals from Ironman training to rehabilitating your injury to get you back to a point where you could run again."

"That's right," responded Peter. "Goals can change as needed, but the important thing is to have them clearly defined as a starting point."

Chapter 13

Continuous Improvement

"True nobility is not about being better than anyone else.
It's about being better than you used to be."
~ Wayne Dwyer ~

Peter was back in Boulder the next quarter so we met for coffee. I began taking notes as I listened to him talk.

"A few years ago I had the opportunity to hear Horst Schulze, President and CEO of Ritz Carlton, speak on the subject of quality and service." began Peter, "Schulze recalled that ten years earlier, even after Ritz was voted the #1 hotel chain, he still rated Ritz as a four on a scale of one to ten. He was concerned that there were no processes in place at Ritz Carlton that guaranteed continuous improvement year after year on the things that were important to guests."

"Continuous improvement is part of the Mid-Atlantic culture," continued Peter. "We are working to continually improve ourselves and the company.

Our business is a transaction business as well as a relationship business. Daily incoming orders, outgoing shipments, new purchases and new parts all add up to complexity and the opportunity for mistakes. Most mistakes are caught internally but several do slip through to our customers. We minimize mistakes by constantly asking ourselves, 'How can we make the business better?' Employees can provide feedback in weekly meetings or stop one of the leaders and talk to him or her. Our culture of trust allows them to communicate what they need and have input into the decision-making process."

He added, "Cross-training throughout the company is a form of continuous improvement that happens regularly and serves to boost employee value and productivity. Today we are doing much more with fewer people because of our focus on training. Training in a new area can be an 'outside of your comfort zone' experience, but the end result is growth and a positive impact."

Peter then told me how feedback from the employees results in new projects and new initiatives every year. He said that some of the very best improvement projects are in the processes that drive employees' day-to-day activities. For example, Mid-Atlantic ships an average of sixty orders per day. At the end of each day, an employee processes an invoice for each order and prints the invoice for mailing the next morning. The Cash-Flow Team began an initiative to email invoices rather than printing and mailing the invoices. The team tracked the initiative's progress and, within a few months, 100% of invoices were being emailed. Besides saving postage and paper expenses, Peter said there was significant timesavings plus the satisfaction of completing a successful improvement project that involved the entire team. He added that twenty-five years ago when he joined the company, it might have taken a week after the shipment was made for the handwritten invoice to get to the customer.

"Our goal is to provide our people with the best equipment to get their jobs done safer, easier and faster," said Peter. "This ties back to our company's mission to care about our employees and treat them like owners."

"I see a similarity with triathlon training," I said. "As an athlete, not only are the training tools and resources available changing with new technologies, but an athlete's body physically changes with training as well.

Athletes need purposeful training plans to avoid becoming stale, injured or over trained. The changes are both gradual and incremental. If there is too much change too soon, an athlete might become injured or fatigued. As a coach, I'm constantly asking my athletes questions like 'How did your swim go?' and 'How did you feel during your race?' I then take the feedback and tweak their plans. Continuous improvement."

"Yes," responded Peter. "This has me thinking about riding a bike as a symbol of continuous improvement. A bike can only go forwards. If you stop moving forward, you fall over. The wheels are continuously moving like the wheels in a person's head keep thinking about how he or she can make things better. Each week, every team at Mid-Atlantic asks, 'What is the one thing we are going to do this week to move things forward?' Continuous improvement is embedded in our culture. We 'walk our talk.' The evidence of this is found in our annual meeting minutes. Last year, our continuous improvement projects totaled fifty-three. It took a page and a half simply to record them."

He continued, "I recently experienced something as a customer that impressed me. It had been a month since I have flown on Southwest Airlines. They are my favorite airline because they really understand how to change processes to 'Wow!' their customers. Before even getting to the airport, the incredibly fast online ordering and check-in process with Southwest prepares the traveler for a wonderful traveling experience. Well, Southwest 'Wowed!' me again. They added barcode readers for smart phones at their check-in counters so that you don't have to print your boarding pass when checking luggage. It may seem insignificant and may not make the news, but it's a big deal to those of us who travel weekly. The lines now move much faster and Southwest saves paper and printing costs. It's a 'win-win' for the airline and their customers. It's continuous improvement around the customers' needs."

I told him how I sell online triathlon training programs for clients who may not want to pay for ongoing coaching. I spent last month rewriting all of my plans to make them easier to understand and follow.

"That's also an example of doing something different than what everyone else is doing," commented Peter. "Continuous improvement is doing the extra things for which there is no penalty for not doing the extra things.

It is focusing on the important but not necessarily urgent. Your plans look very professional. I really like the customized approach and the pictures in your training guide. That's what the world wants. I see it every day. Cindy told me that she drove fifty-seven miles for a haircut this weekend. The salon pampered her with attention and she sat in a massage chair while her hair was being washed and conditioned. It's something that no other salon does. That's the 'Wow!' in her experience."

He added, "The very best kinds of continuous improvement are those that have a positive impact on your customers or, better yet, your customer's customers. I remember attending our semi-annual fall conference when Katie was around ten years old. The conference dates conflicted with Halloween making it impossible for me to take Katie 'trick-or-treating.' At the end of the conference, I completed a survey and recommended a date change so that families would not miss this special time with their kids. The company changed the dates of the next conference and Halloween has been protected ever since."

Peter continued, "When I first joined Mid-Atlantic, we were a commodity company treating every customer, supplier and employee the same. Now we treat everyone the way they want to be treated. We are nimble and have created flexible, fast processes because we recognize the importance of continuously improving around the customer's needs. The results are finding their way to our bottom line. None of this would be possible without a focus on continuous improvement."

Chapter 14

Processes and Prevention

"It's not that I'm so smart, it's just that I stay with problems longer."
~ Albert Einstein ~

"Tell me more about the processes at Mid-Atlantic Rubber," I asked Peter during a phone conversation a few weeks later. "You said Mid-Atlantic's culture of continuous improvement is enabled through processes. What are the processes you put in place?"

"At Mid-Atlantic," Peter said, "we follow the *7 Habits* process which aligns with our core principle of interdependence, a team process, which aligns with our core principle of focus and the ISO 9002 process, which aligns to our core principle of prevention."

Peter explained that ISO 9002 is an industry standard created by the International Organization for Standardization. Its long name is the model for quality assurance in production, installation and servicing.

"Obtaining our ISO 9002 certification was a huge company-wide continuous improvement initiative in and of itself," he said, "Training is a huge element in our ISO procedures. Our goal is to anticipate problems before they happen. We document the issues and put processes in place to prevent them in the future."

I asked him about what business was like before ISO 9002 certification.

He replied, "We lost so much business because we didn't have processes or procedures in place to deal with customer complaints or a way to prevent errors from happening again. When we first implemented the ISO 9002 system in 1997, the employees hated it because the processes took so much extra time. The system required documenting everything. Now, everyone knows about a problem before it happens. Things happen faster because we have a process and that has made us so much more responsive to customers and able to perform so much better. If an employee changes positions, someone else could pick up their job seamlessly because of training they've already had."

Peter explained that in his early days at Mid-Atlantic, each sales person would record the details of a customer phone call on a yellow pad in a set format, a simple form of a process. As Mid-Atlantic acquired more and more customers and salespeople, the company needed a more integrated approach that was transparent to all and allowed for the collection and documentation of valuable data (the 'gold') from each call. When the company implemented a CRM (customer relationship management) software system, employees could capture the gold and much more. Peter said that customer information is now filed under a customer or supplier code and accessible by any employee for follow up, ongoing sales and customer service.

I asked Peter for a specific example of a process that Mid-Atlantic implemented.

He said, "I'll use the Warehouse Team as an example. We have inventory on-site in the warehouse, in three storage containers in the parking lot and in off-site storage at a truck depot. Prior to implementing a process to barcode incoming inventory, we would experience lost parts daily, often resulting in poor service to our customers. The parts shown on the inventory cards were often wrong more than right, thus reducing our productivity and ability to take an order without calling the customer back."

"Now," he continued, "our process is to triple check everything coming into our building before it goes into our computer and onto our shelves as inventory. The Warehouse Team checks in each shipment against existing orders. If there is no order for a particular part, then the part goes into inventory. Parts are stored in a certain area and parts for certain companies are kept in certain locations. For example, areas D, E and F are specific locations for two of our largest customers. The most often needed parts are stored lower and more easily accessible on shelves while the less needed parts are stored higher."

Peter explained that when shipping an order out to a customer, one of the warehouse employees prints out the order, looks up the weight on the load and then compares the weight on the load to the weight on the order to see if they match. The employee also checks parts against part numbers. There is then a second check by another person who then puts labels on the boxes for shipping so UPS can pick them up.

"Our parts are used in many applications, some of which we will never even know," Peter said. "There is a potential liability and added expense for us if we provide the wrong or defective part to a customer. With our current processes, we know that the orders to our customers will be right. We also never again have to take a year-end physical inventory and our cycle count accuracy is consistently over 99%."

I told him that it sounded like there was a lot of work up-front to set up and document the processes, but, in the long run, the processes saved the company time and money while improving customer satisfaction.

"Absolutely," he replied. "We identified what's important to our customers— on time and accurate delivery—and put the processes in place to meet their needs. The key is to continually improve your business around the needs of your customers. The ISO 9002 motto is to document what you do, do what you document. We do that."

"Can there be too many processes?" I wondered.

"Well, it really boils down to more safety checks and fewer errors, just like the carpenter's saying to measure twice and cut once," Peter replied.

"We only had eleven shipping errors out of more than 15,000 transactions last year."

"That's incredible," I said. "When I was the organizer of the Luray Triathlon in Virginia, I had to depend on a core staff of about a dozen people plus hundreds of volunteers to help make the race a fun and safe event for the participants. One important process that we put in place for the week after the race was to meet with key race personnel, local town officials, police and rescue organizations to discuss what went well and what things needed to improve for next year while the event was still fresh in everyone's minds. We collected and documented feedback from this meeting and from the athletes so that when the next year came around, we knew what we needed to do to make the race better. It was a simple thing to hold the meeting and ask for feedback, but this simple thing enabled the race to continuously improve each year."

"Yes," said Peter. "It's all about putting the proper processes in place."

"Having the proper processes in place," I added, "reminds me of a saying from the special forces: 'Slow is smooth. Smooth is fast.' In other words, if you do things right the first time, even if slower, you'll still be faster in the end."

Chapter 15

Planning & Measuring

"What's measured improves."
~ Peter Drucker ~

"How do you manage everything going on in your personal life?" I asked Peter over lunch during his next visit to Colorado. "You lead a company. You're also a sales representative for another company. You're on the road nearly every week to either visit Katie, travel for work or to travel to your beach house. On top of all that, you're training for an Ironman which requires time, focus and dedication. How do you do it? How do you fit everything in?"

"What if you had an extra hour each day so that there were 25 hours in a day?" Peter asked me back. "What would you do with the extra 365 hours in a year?"

I shrugged, "I would probably try to do more."

Peter smiled, "The reality is that there are only twenty-four hours in a day. However, when you stay focused on your highest priorities, you will have the impact of an extra hour each day. The single best thing you can do each week is weekly planning. I do it every Sunday night. I start by looking at my mission statement. Then, I review my roles, and my goals per role, and ask myself, 'What is the most important thing that I could do this week in each role that would make the most difference?' I end up with five or six things to add to my 'to do' list in addition to other tasks and appointments I have scheduled."

"What do you mean by roles," I asked.

He explained, "Roles have to do with relationships, including my relationship with myself. Each of my roles in my life affects someone else. For me, my major roles are: husband, father, CEO, sales rep, triathlete and mentor. I have written tribute statements for each role. A tribute statement is basically what I would like the key people in my life to say about me when I'm old. Consider this an invite for you to come to my 80th birthday party. I will let you know where and when or Kathy will let you know if it's a surprise. I am giving you plenty of notice just in case you are in California or Hawaii."

I smiled.

Peter continued, "Weekly planning is a process and is something that most people won't take the time to do so I know it is the right thing to do. I also keep a 'red journal' of my accomplishments for the month. During my weekly planning session, I record my accomplishments for the prior week. I have one page for personal accomplishments and one page for business accomplishments. I end up with ten to fifteen accomplishments on each page for the week. I also start each month with a master list of key accomplishments that I would like to get done during that month for each role."

"I often finish a week and feel like I haven't accomplished anything," I said. "I like your idea of tracking accomplishments in a journal."

"I now have several years of accomplishments to look back on," Peter said. "It's really neat when I can look back and see what I have accomplished and know that most of it supports my mission statement and the people who are the key relationships in my life. I record beach weekends with Kathy, track meets to support Katie, every sales call I make, conferences that I attend, races I do, our trip to Boulder, etc."

"The same principle holds true for triathlon," I added. "When I work with a coaching client like you, I will call or email you to talk about your training for the next two weeks. We'll look at what you've accomplished in the past two weeks and talk about any obstacles or challenges. Because you've logged your workouts into your training log, we can objectively measure whether you met your goals or not. Then with your input, I'll put together a detailed plan for you for the next two weeks."

"That's essentially what we do at Mid-Atlantic, too," replied Peter. "We kick off each week with a one hour meeting to identify key activities for the coming week. We look at month-to-date and year-to-date results on all of the goals we set at our annual planning session so we know exactly where we are relative to our goals. My expectation is that every employee at Mid-Atlantic starts each week with a weekly plan, too. It's a work in progress. Most employees don't do it as well as they would like to do it because it takes time and some don't have a mission statement or written goals. There is a still room for improvement in this area. I do feel good, however, that we are modeling weekly planning at the company level. I may make weekly planning the focus of our next quarter's training."

"One more thought regarding triathlon coaching," I said. "Instead of evaluating detailed financial reports like at Mid-Atlantic, as a coach and client, we can evaluate your progress through fitness tests. Every week, you time yourself on the same four-mile run course around your neighborhood. You established a benchmark that you can then compare against for future runs. So far this year, you've dramatically dropped your time from more than forty minutes a run to less than thirty-six minutes."

"Great example," commented Peter. "Having a plan in place and measuring against it are necessary components towards achieving goals."

Chapter 16

Sometimes the Magic Doesn't Work

"Let me embrace thee, sour adversity, for wise men say it is the wisest course."
~ William Shakespeare ~

I was frustrated. Since the previous summer, I had been working on a new business idea for an online triathlon school that I had planned to launch on January 1. It was now February and I had no idea when I would be able to launch the business.

Peter emailed me:

> You and I talk about this all the time: "Learn by doing." And you are always doing and taking action, trying new things. Keep your faith, David. I have kept my faith for 22 years that everything would work out for my ownership of Mid-Atlantic. On Monday afternoon at 4 PM, I received Clarence's stock shares making me the sole owner of the company. What a moment!

I will celebrate with Kathy maybe this weekend, as we reflect on our journey from Singapore and the faith that it took to leave our jobs on a promise and a handshake. So much of a new journey begins with vision, passion and faith.

I use my example as a teaching lesson to Katie as she begins her next journey to graduate school and then ultimately her career. Katie will be successful because she is principle-centered, other-focused and has a tremendous support team. This reminds me of when she used to bowl with bumpers raised up in the gutters so that the ball always knocked down some pins. That's what principles and a support system do. I, too, will ultimately be successful with my Kona goal because I am principle-centered, other-focused and have a great support system. Thanks for all you do for me. The future is abundant and is exciting for both of us.

"You have lots of success stories at Mid-Atlantic and in your life," I said to Peter during our call, "It's almost magical."

"Yes, I sometimes think that making the right choices and embracing change creates that magic. But, sometimes the magic doesn't always work," said Peter. "I'll give you an example. Mid-Atlantic's business runs on inventory. Because of long lead times to acquire parts, we want parts readily available on the shelf when a customer calls. Inventory management and planning is a process that we never have successfully implemented."

Peter explained that inventory management and planning is the how the company forecasts, plans and buys to minimize inventory while maximizing customer service levels. Because Mid-Atlantic is a distributor, customers expect Mid-Atlantic to have parts in stock when they want them. Managing inventory is tricky because there are more than 1,200 parts and at least that many customers.

Peter continued, "We don't use an inventory planning system so our ordering is very much based on a manual effort requiring lots of reports and analysis. In 2008 we invested heavily in new 'state-of-the-art' planning software. The software had some real nice features and—in theory—would help us improve purchasing by looking at past data so that we could order more efficiently for the next year. We spent more than $30,000 on the software before finally pulling the plug two years later when we realized that it would not meet our goal to minimize our inventory while maximizing service levels to our customers."

"Why did the software fail?" I asked.

Peter answered, "When the economy dipped in 2009, customers cut back on their orders. Because the software had already ordered parts based on the prior year's order, we had ordered too much—and we couldn't turn off the spigot. In hindsight, planning software might have worked if the economy had remained more stable."

He added, "When we installed the software initially, we also had to run our old system in parallel, which created duplicative work for our employees. We spent days and nights with the software company and paid for their people to fly to and from Mid-Atlantic. The software never worked the way it was supposed to work. The software company was a classic case of 'overpromise and under deliver' that cost Mid-Atlantic a lot of time and money. We eventually disengaged from the planning software and ended up making upgrades to our existing software."

I remembered some of my own experiences. "I've been involved in a number of technology projects when I worked at corporations. Inevitably, the projects always took longer and cost more than originally anticipated due to unforeseen situations. During my last project, my company backed out of an initial agreement with a vendor after we discovered that the vendor couldn't deliver the functionality as promised without significant development costs. So we switched to another vendor because someone had the foresight to recognize the long-term benefits would outweigh the costs already spent on the first vendor."

Peter nodded. "Relationships can break down, too. The landlord for the Mid-Atlantic building also owned a small manufacturing company involved in the die cutting of gaskets. He planted an idea in my head one day that he would like to sell his business to me because it was a complementary business to Mid-Atlantic and only fifteen miles away. We met to discuss and soon after had an agreement for me to purchase the business with the majority of financing held by him. My upfront investment was a down payment and the legal fees associated with the purchase agreement."

Peter shared that a week before closing the deal, a key employee of the gasket business unexpectedly died in his sleep. To Peter's disappointment, the owner canceled the deal, explaining that the reason he was selling the business was because his daughter and this key employee could not get along. Because the key employee was gone, there was no need for him to sell the business. He would simply turn it over to his daughter.

"That sucks," I commented.

"As the saying goes," he said, "when one door closes, another one opens. That was the case with this deal. With money in hand and a purchase agreement that could easily be modified, I offered to buy the building that Mid-Atlantic occupied instead of continuing to lease it. Several months later, we purchased a couple of die-cutting machines and began a small manufacturing operation of our own. Looking back, I am convinced that our growth over the years would not have been possible without the purchase of this building."

I reflected, "Sometimes the magic does eventually work."

Chapter 17

Have a Coach; Be a Coach

"Coaching is a profession of love. You can't coach people unless you love them."
~ Eddie Robinson ~

Peter began our next call, "One of the best bosses I ever had was a guy named Rob, who was the first of many bosses during my fifteen years at Data General Corporation. Rob was the purchasing manager and I was one of six buyers supporting a 400,000 square foot manufacturing facility. At work, Rob was a great leader and mentor. Outside of work, he was passionate about golf and shot par on most rounds. I knew the game of golf from my childhood but never really played or took lessons, as I preferred to be in the swimming pool. Rob changed all of that for me when he gave me my very first set of clubs and spent countless hours with me on the course and at the driving range. Rob had a family but somehow found the extra time to coach me in golf. I became addicted to golf and enjoyed every minute I could spend on the course."

He continued, "There are many life lessons found in the game of golf, but for me, the lesson I took away was how great I felt being coached by Rob. The experience made me want to 'pay it forward' and coach someone else like Rob coached me. What I discovered was that it felt as great to coach others as it did to be coached."

"Maybe that's why I never really became interested in the game of golf," I replied. "I never had a coach like Rob."

"Having a coach does make a difference," continued Peter. He then shared a story about how Cindy's exercise group began working with inner city middle school kids as part of the President's Physical Fitness Program to promote fitness in schools.

Cindy was Mid-Atlantic's Comptroller who managed the Cash-Flow Team. She was hired in 1990 to be Mid-Atlantic's bookkeeper. She was one of many applicants but the only one to pass the profile test provided by Mid-Atlantic's accounting firm. Cindy was a single mom with lots of bookkeeping experience. According to Peter, she quickly showed that she was much more than a bookkeeper. Cindy was a people-person and a problem solver and Mid-Atlantic had no shortage of problems to solve.

Peter began, "These kids were all under-achievers failing out of school. The school required the kids to enroll in an after school program and most of the kids did not want to be there. They were also at the age where they felt like they knew it all. The kids were tested on sit-ups, push-ups and the one-mile run. At the beginning of the program, not a single kid could run a mile."

He continued, "By the end of the program, every kid could run a mile under twelve minutes. Cindy was amazed to see the kids get better and better each week, and she said it felt good to coach them. Recognition was so very important to the kids. They didn't care what they received and at the end they wanted to be in the program."

I asked him about my coaching of him for triathlon.

"I had my personal best time at Ironman Lake Placid in 2009, the first year you began coaching me," he replied, "That was also the first year that I was able to successfully complete two Ironman races in a single year. It was a great year for me and since that time, I have reflected on what role your coaching had on my performance. I have concluded that I could not have done it one my own."

"How so?" I asked curiously.

"Your design of the workouts tailored to my schedule, my capabilities and my goals was as important as the accountability that your coaching provided. More than anything, your feedback and constant encouragement were the external force I needed to keep going. My other insight about coaching was an eye opener for me: *I will always perform much better for someone else than I will perform for myself.*"

"That's a good insight," I said.

"Your belief in me was what made the difference," he continued. "If you thought that I could do it, then I knew I could do it. It did not matter what I thought initially. Any negative self-talk inside of me was overridden by your confidence in me. You are constantly encouraging me to do new things and to better believe in myself. This is what gives me 100% confidence that despite being a MORAG, my term for a middle of the road age grouper, I will eventually earn a slot to compete at Kona. Everyone needs to have a great coach and not just for triathlons."

"So what are the characteristics of a good coach?" I asked.

Peter thought for a moment then said, "Like leaders, coaches care. Good coaches make the time to really get to know their clients by listening intently to better understand them. What a coach will discover is other ways that he or she can help (maybe for free) and, in doing so, develop a more enduring relationship and long-term loyalty. A good coach learns what someone wants to accomplish and why they want to accomplish it. Then, the coach helps him or her take the steps to achieve the goal. The coach provides regular doses of positive feedback, a lot of encouragement and skills building. The coach sends signals saying 'I believe in you' and 'You can do it.' This is what parents, teachers and great bosses do all the time."

Peter shared an email that Kathy had sent to Katie the morning before Katie's cross-country meet:

Good morning! It is a great day!! It is YOUR race day!! I am so confident in what you can do at this conference. You have worked hard for three years. I watched as you shaved over 30 seconds off your time in cross-country in the first two meets. And I saw you keep up with your team. You are ready for this. Give it your all. Give it your best. You will achieve a personal best and you will do what the coach knows you can do. Believe in yourself!!!!! Go in there saying: I AM GOING TO DO THIS!!! I am so proud of you!!!! Can't wait to see you run!!

I love you. Mom

"That's a nice email," I said.

Peter said, "Even coaches need coaches. Imagine what the world might be like if everyone was a great coach to someone else! We all have something that we are passionate about or something that we do great, something that we could teach to others. In fact, I have a theory that most of our problems can be solved by the very people around us, if we just take the time to engage with others."

"How do you think coaching fits with leadership?" I asked.

Peter answered, "Because coaching is what great leaders do. They develop the next generation of leaders. Maybe it's working with middle school kids or mentoring a new employee at work. Maybe it's helping a neighbor. There are no shortages of coaching opportunities. Do you remember the boss, friend or teacher that influenced you the most? We can all be that person to someone else."

Peter continued, "I like what Zig Ziglar, world famous sales motivator, said 'You can have anything you want in life as long as you help enough other people get what they want.' People don't always coach to get something monetary in return, but coaches always get a lot in return. Plus, it feels good to help others solve their problems or to help others become better at something. Finding a coach does not need to cost a lot of money. Besides a fast track to improvement, you also learn skills and tools that you can use to help others. Life is short. Hire a coach and become a coach. See a difference in yourself and make a difference to someone else."

I commented, "I may be your triathlon coach, but you are coaching me, too."

"It's funny, David," said Peter, "I only recently had this paradigm shift that we learn best by teaching others. This book really is a great teaching and coaching tool. It is my hope that many people of all ages will read this book and pass on the key points to others. I wish someone had shared some of these points with me when I was eighteen years old."

When I think back through the years I've known Peter, our relationship has evolved from a simple coach and athlete relationship to a deeper relationship across many aspects of our lives. Peter is also a friend, a mentor and a role model for being positive. I know that I'm a better person than when I first met Peter. Peter has that effect.

Chapter 18

Relationships Are Key

Coming together is a beginning.
Keeping together is progress.
Working together is success.
~ Henry Ford ~

I had traveled from Colorado back east to Virginia in August to produce the Luray Triathlon then spent a few days afterward with Peter at his beach house on Maryland's eastern shore.

"Tell me about John Vargo," I asked. I had watched John coach and encourage Peter through his swim workouts one morning.

"John has been my swim coach every Tuesday at 5:30 am for over fifteen years," Peter began. "He focuses on me for the entire hour. I know this because he walks alongside me every lap—that's 80 laps each week. He even walked alongside when he had a foot injury from a running race."

"Fifteen years?" I said. "Wow. That says a lot about your relationship with John if you've worked with him for that long."

"My relationship with John is built on trust," Peter replied, "I trust that he understands my goals and will present workouts to me to support my goals and my principles. He gives me drills and exercises that I can do on my own when I am not with him. As I have aged, he has given me new drills to do to stay strong and to be more flexible. He has also only canceled one appointment and that was because he had an emergency appendix operation. John has completed marathons and Ironmans himself so he understands the training required for the sport. My relationship with John is an example of him following the Platinum Rule."

"What do you mean by the Platinum Rule?" I asked.

Peter answered, "People and companies want to be treated the way they want to be treated—not necessarily the way that everyone else is being treated. Stephen Covey taught that relationships are like bank accounts. You make deposits and withdrawals that either build upon the relationship or takes away from it. Ask, what's my balance with a person? Is it positive or negative? Is it high trust or low trust?'"

"I like the analogy," I said. "Doing something nice for someone is a deposit while doing something negative or selfish is a withdrawal."

"Yes," replied Peter. "In the end, it boils down to 'win-win' thinking. It takes specially trained people who are well grounded in their own principles to first think about what's a win for the other person rather than only a win for their own personal gain. But, it's not enough to give. It's unconditional giving that makes a difference. Be other-focused rather than self-focused."

He continued, "Mid-Atlantic's company charter implies building high trust relationships. This is the cornerstone of all that Mid-Atlantic stands for. Customer relationships, family relationships, employee relationships, supplier relationships and even our spiritual relationships all hinge on perfecting the 'R' word."

"So what do you think is the key to successful relationships?" I asked him.

He replied, "A close friend once told me that the key to successful relationships is sacrifice. Sacrifice is the component that shows people how much you care. People want to do business with people that care. Caring comes in a lot of forms, but caring begins by being connected. Connecting involves an investment in time, maybe even unpaid. I like the saying: 'People don't care how much you know until they know how much you care.' Love is spelled T-I-M-E."

I asked him for an example.

He said, "If I am tired when I come home but spend quality time with my daughter rather than lay on the couch, I am building a better relationship with my daughter. Getting up early to read or exercise rather than sleeping an extra hour helps me have a better relationship with myself. There are countless examples of things we do and don't do for ourselves and significant others that help to move our relationships in the right or wrong direction."

He continued, "We get lots of help with our relationships during May, June, July and August. MotheR's Day, FatheR's Day, wateRmelon, cRabs, tRips togetheR, wateR paRks, RolleRcoasteRs, hambuRgeRs on the gRill, conceRts, summeR walks, longeR days, Roses, waRmeR weatheR, etc. There are lots of 'R' activities during these four months. That is why there is no letter 'R' in the names of these months. But as we end August, we head into the eight-month cycle of months with the letter 'R.' Most people think these are the good months for oysters. My theory about months with the letter 'R' is different. I believe these are the months that require us to pay close attention to the quality of our key relationships. There can be lots of stress during this eight month period with school, traffic, lines, holidays, ice, snow, bills, more bills, taxes, etc. Because there are a lot fewer 'R' activities to bring us together during these months, we really have to focus more on our relationships during this period."

"How about a business example?" I asked.

"The really great companies have figured out how to customize their service offerings," replied Peter. "At Mid-Atlantic, our leaders model the behaviors we want our employees to give to our customers. We treat our employees like owners and focus on what we can do to help them. They can do the same thing with our clients and suppliers."

He continued, "One of our largest customers called Mid-Atlantic on a July 4th holiday weekend and said they needed parts immediately. The initial order that they had placed was for delivery in August so we did not have the parts yet in inventory. Our sales manager reached out to our factory in China to see if the factory could deliver the parts more quickly. He then asked the factory to fly the parts as fast as possible to the customer. The factory said the parts would be there on Tuesday. The sales manager called the frantic customer at home to tell him about the parts and gave him the tracking number."

I asked him how the customer responded.

"The customer was amazed," Peter said, "Within twelve hours of the initial frantic call, the customer's cataclysmic meltdown was solved. Mid-Atlantic also ate the additional cost of shipping. We could have stuck the customer with the cost but that might have created tension later and hurt our relationship."

He continued, "As our sales manager likes to say, 'The customer is always the customer. We become extremely important when something leaks, squeaks or shakes across the floor. And when something leaks, squeaks or shakes across the floor, we want them to call us first.' We want our customers to remain our customers by building, strengthening and continually renewing the relationships. As such, we love customer feedback—the good, bad and ugly. If we get that feedback, then we know what our customer is thinking about and what pains they have now so we can now work to help them fix their pain."

Finding the right balance as a triathlete, especially with regards to relationships with other people, is something I've struggled with over the years. I knew many triathletes who also struggled with finding that balance, too. I asked Peter how he was able to spend quality time with Kathy and Katie while managing one company, doing sales for another company and training for an Ironman.

He responded, "I think Kathy is the best person to answer that question. I'll have her email you."

A few days later Kathy emailed me her answer:

Over 25 years ago, I was so fortunate to marry the most dedicated, hard working, goal driven and ambitious man that I have ever met. I have watched him go from the challenge of a marathon to triathlons and now Ironman competitions. I am confident and look forward to the day he achieves the qualifying time that will take him to Kona. To see Peter accomplish his goal after all of his hard work, strength, determination and countless years of training (and injuries) to participate in the ultimate challenge of this elite race would give me such a great sense of pride and joy. I still cry (both joy and fear) every time I see the start of the Ironman in Lake Placid.

Traveling to his many races has made for some wonderful vacations and family times. Being a cheerleader has become a challenge in itself as we map out course locations to catch a glimpse or track races through target times. Being around all the athletes, their families and the many wonderful personal stories in each race have only made for some great life's lessons and the creation of a new athlete in our family—Katie.

However, the years of training and competitions have not been without a few bumps along the road in our family life. The hours of training have definitely been a challenge for Peter as a father and a husband. Balancing his time has been difficult and I have taken on many roles that normally would have been shared by Peter. The 'honey-do' list tends to be long and there are times where I really feel overwhelmed, but I am pretty good at multitasking, so everything gets done.

I tease both Katie and Peter about being high maintenance with their diets, every new fad that Peter tries to improve his performance with, taveling to multiple training sites each day and of course all the massages. Extremely early workouts lead to early bedtimes and a husband who can fall asleep in mid conversation or anywhere. Training hours also equate to work hours at home. So even though Peter is here, he is in his office catching up with the demands of work requirements. Weekends are for long runs and long bikes so there is limited free time with the family or for us as a couple.

I asked her to explain more about how she handled the challenges. She emailed back:

Communication and patience are two things that come to mind. When Katie is home, we have Sunday dinners that end with a family meeting. We have made it a tradition that is memorialized with a book that records our past week and goals for the upcoming week as well as the problems to be addressed. We then close with a compliment to each other. It has been fun to look back over the years and see what our lives looked like. Now that Katie is in college, we still have weekly 'calendar' meetings, to make sure we are in sync with each other and know our schedules. Information is wonderful and there are less conflicts when there are no surprises!

We travel a lot for both Peter and Katie's competitions and our dog, Rudy, has taken on the nickname of 'Gypsy Dog.' We try to make our trips fun and like mini-vacations. We set one night a week aside for 'date night' to make sure that we know that our marriage is still a priority. And of course I keep Peter's 'honey do' list updated with one of the items always being to 'Kiss Kathy!' Peter never fails to make me tea in the morning and leaves a special note before he leaves for his early swim workouts.

"What advice you give to the spouse of an athlete in training for the Ironman?" I asked back.

She answered:

Keep your eye on the prize. It is not always easy and sometimes the sacrifices may be tough, but the rewards are great. I have seen Peter use his workouts as an outlet for stress, to improve his health, feel better about himself and feel a sense of accomplishment at the finish of each race.

His training helps him to be a better person and better spouse and father...if that were ever possible. I knew what I was getting into when I married him and these challenges have turned into great rewards.

Be patient and keep the lines of communication open. Life is not always easy, but these are the times that make for some incredible memories!

I asked Peter if there was anything that he would add about the impact of triathlons on his life.

He replied, "I tend to be an extremely positive person so I tend to look at everything with a positive and optimistic slant. Triathlon is mostly training which means I do some form of exercise six days a week, which has really been good for my health and has had a positive impact on my daughter. As Kathy mentioned in her email, we have gone places and done things because of triathlons that we otherwise would not have done. Triathlon is a healthy lifestyle. On the business side, triathlon taught me more about goal setting and strategic planning. Long-range goals need to be broken down into smaller goals. Triathlon taught me that mental toughness is as important as physical endurance. The mind, how and what you think about, can often be the difference maker. Getting better does not just happen; it requires action. Triathlon has taught me the importance of being proactive in everything I do. Similar with being proactive is the idea of taking initiative. In business, we develop new initiatives every year, just as I do to help me improve in triathlons. "

"Can you tell me a little more about your relationship with Kathy?" I asked.

Peter replied, "Kathy and I were married October 26, 1985. We traveled and had the time of our lives for five years. We held hands and kissed each other well after our honeymoon was over. Family members would always kid us to cut it out. When Katie was born in 1990, we settled down from traveling. We stopped holding each other's hand because we were now each holding one of Katie's hands. After Katie went off to college in 2008, Kathy and I became really close again, even holding hands. We depend on each other and are truly best friends. We are still having the time of our lives."

Chapter 19
Building Relationships

"Don't walk behind me; I may not lead. Don't walk in front of me;
I may not follow. Just walk beside me and be my friend."
~ Albert Camus ~

Peter and I were meeting again in a coffee shop in Boulder when he was back in town.

Peter began: "In our busy, hectic lives, we come into contact with dozens of people per day but seldom do we really take the time to connect with many, if any. In my experience, a simple 'Hello,' a question, a smile or a compliment are rare. Maybe we are scared, embarrassed, shy, in a rush or one of any number of hundreds of other reasons why we don't connect. Grocery stores, airplanes, sporting events, restaurants, the telephone, etc.—there are no shortages of opportunities to connect with others."

He continued, "When I was pumping gas one Saturday afternoon, I smiled at the man at the pump next to me and asked him, 'How do you like your car?' He returned the smile, introduced himself as Charlie and began talking about his car. The conversation quickly moved to him asking me if I was a runner. I had just finished my long run looking like 'something the cat dragged in.' Besides being the former coach for the Villanova Track Team, Charlie had won a gold medal at the 1956 Olympics for the 400-meter run and lived in my hometown. The story is even more ironic because my running coach had moved to California on Friday. I hope to track—no pun intended—Charlie down again and get to know him and better learn from his life experiences as an Olympic runner, coach and father."

Peter added, "There is a greeting in India 'Tashi deley,' which can be translated to mean, 'I honor the greatness in you.' I made a resolution that day to 'honor the greatness in others' by acknowledging others, no matter how busy I was. You just never know who you might meet, what you might learn or what impact you might have on someone else, just as Charlie did on me."

"How about relationships between businesses?" I asked.

Peter replied, "Mid-Atlantic's largest supplier is Lord Corporation." Peter explained that Lord is a one billion dollar company with a different culture than Mid-Atlantic. Mid-Atlantic has a written contract with Lord that identifies what each company will do for each other. The contract is like a set of rules with procedures and guidelines.

Peter continued, "The Lord relationship is simple. We look at Lord as one of our best customers even though they are our largest supplier. How is that for a paradigm change?"

"So Lord is also a customer because they count on you to sell their parts?" I asked.

"Yes," said Peter. "From the beginning of our distributor relationship with Lord, it was clear that the relationship would far exceed what we had come to expect from past supplier relationships. Lord initially gave us a generous amount of customer business and then doubled it several years later. They continue to turn over house accounts to us. Lord's product line required a higher level of technical engineering knowledge than our other products, but Lord was able to provide our sales reps with the necessary training. Lord also invited us to their annual sales meetings and training programs. The lines of communication between us were clearly open and Lord demonstrated a willingness to listen to our needs and provide us with the necessary information. The better informed we all were, the better the partnership worked."

"What made the relationship work so well?" I asked.

He answered, "Our partnership developed and thrived from a relationship based on trust—there's the trust word again. In so many ways, we look at Lord more as a customer than a vendor as we sought to provide solutions for them. This mutual trust, combined with business advantages, has kept us faithful to the exclusiveness of distributorship. Over the years, we've resisted any temptations to use overseas rubber sources to make cheaper versions of products in Lord's line even if the price difference would have won us the business. We'd rather pass up an opportunity than jeopardize our relationship with Lord."

Peter continued, "The customers we serve on behalf of Lord range from the individual who buys twenty dollars worth of mounts each year for a tractor to a large tow truck manufacturer. The tow truck company is an example of our Lord partnership at work. They became our customer because they were in the distribution territory given to us by Lord. Lord has worked very closely with us to help build the business that the customer does with us. Our Lord sales numbers have grown steadily each year with this customer since we began working with them in 1995. Even more, our relationship with this customer opened the door for opportunities to provide additional solutions to them through our die cut and custom molded capabilities."

Peter shared that there were other fringe benefits in working with Lord. For example, when Mid-Atlantic was working towards earning its ISO 9002 certification, Lord's existing ISO 9002 certification documentation provided Mid-Atlantic with examples to use in developing its own policies and procedures. He then explained how Mid-Atlantic reciprocated back to Lord when Lord developed a new product line that came out of research and development. Mid-Atlantic helped with the sales and marketing of the new product line by putting their products on Mid-Atlantic's website and selling them online to anyone in the world.

I asked Peter about building personal relationships.

He answered, "We fired our mobile dog groomer after she came to our house a year ago and I witnessed her harsh behavior towards, Rudy. She was verbally abusive to him. It was no wonder Rudy was scared, traumatized and wanted to eat her for lunch every time she came to the house. Since then for the past year, Kathy has been driving thirty minutes at 6:30 AM on the first Tuesday of each month to get Rudy's hair cut and toenails clipped. Rudy's groomer comes in early before any other dogs are there so that Rudy can be more at ease. How's that for customizing a service around the special needs of a customer?"

"That's awesome," I said.

Peter continued, "Rudy is still frightened but really likes his new groomer. This past weekend, we had to put Rudy on some medicine for a leg problem. He was doing better so Kathy took him for his normal Tuesday appointment. She cautioned the groomer to be sensitive to his leg because he had been having problems with it. The groomer stopped and said, 'We have come so far over the past year with Rudy. Why don't we skip the session today? His hair looks fine and I don't want to take a chance of having him not trust me.' The groomer turned away money in favor of doing the right thing and not impacting the relationship she built with Rudy. As a result, she has really increased her relationship with Kathy."

Chapter 20
Being Other-focused

"True happiness…is not obtained through self-gratification,
but through fidelity to a worthy purpose."
~ *Helen Keller* ~

Peter began our phone call, "I will never forget Keyoko not only because of his name, but also because of his service. Keyoko is a 6'3" waiter at the Hilton restaurant where Bill, Cindy and I met for most of our quarterly Friday morning meetings. Our routine was fairly predictable, including Cindy asking for blueberry pancakes and the waiter telling her that they were not available that day. Cindy had ordered blueberry pancakes one summer when the restaurant was running a special but the restaurant had not offered blueberry pancakes since. On this particular morning, it looked like it would be a similar experience for Cindy as Keyoko took our order and promptly informed Cindy that blueberry pancakes were not available. Cindy expressed her normal disappointment and ordered the regular pancakes."

Peter, continued, "Can you imagine the look on Cindy's face fifteen minutes later when Keyoko came back with a stack of the best looking blueberry pancakes? Keyoko smiled at Cindy and told her, 'I pulled some strings for you in the kitchen.' What he really meant was that he listened to her and cared enough to do what it took to please her as his customer. The irony of this story is that up until our Keyoko experience, most of our other service experiences at this restaurant had been less than average. We had actually started looking for a new restaurant at which to meet. Keyoko changed our perception of the restaurant with a single stack of blueberry pancakes. The message I took away from this is to listen with understanding and caring for opportunities to 'Wow!' customers. Let's give customers something to brag about. That's what being other-focused is about."

I said, "Something so simple. I know there are plenty of opportunities for me to do a better job helping my coaching clients."

Peter smiled, "I can give you many examples of great customer service stories, but we can all learn from our bad service experiences as well."

Peter shared how Bill and Cindy experienced poor customer service after they purchased a used travel trailer. Bill took the trailer to a dealer for service and to attach an outside grill. Upon inspection, the dealer suggested that Bill have the floor replaced since the floor was still under warranty with the manufacturer. Bill agreed and left the trailer with the dealer to complete the work.

Two weeks passed and the dealer had not done any work. Two more weeks and the work was still not done. After another week, Bill began making calls to the dealer and then to the manufacturer. The manufacturer finally told Bill that the dealer did not have the interest or the capability to replace the floor. In fact, the dealer had not even touched the trailer during the six week period and never called Bill to let him know that they were not working on it. When Bill went to pick up the trailer, management never apologized and there was a lot of finger pointing. As a final act, the dealer pulled the wrong trailer from the lot and tried to give it to Bill.

"In reflection," Peter said, "Bill believed that the dealer's management team was weak, which in turn trickled down to the rest of the employees and resulted in the current company culture. A company culture, good or bad, permeates through the entire business. Great service begins with open, honest communication, which was clearly lacking from this service inter-action. It's tough to move towards trust if the management team is stuck in rust."

I replied. "I've never experienced anything quite that bad, but I have acquired new clients who had had bad customer service experiences with other coaches. I'm amazed at how appreciative future clients are when I respond to their email questions within a day of the email. Do other coaches simply ignore their clients?"

"It happens more than you would think," said Peter. "I've told you many times that I try to do the opposite of the things that most people do. Make a difference by being different. This also includes going to the extra effort—in other words, being exceptional. I'll give you an example. I love surprises almost as much as first time experiences and happy endings."

Peter shared, "Cindy always noticed and joked about me holding the paper I was reading far out in front of me. One day Cindy invited me to lunch. We left at 12:30 PM with Cindy driving. We had driven five miles when she pulled into a hospital parking lot. Cindy said she needed to pick up a prescription. Minutes later, we were in an eye doctor's office for my 1 PM appointment to have my eyes examined—or my arms lengthened as Cindy joked to the receptionist. I was fitted for reading glasses in lieu of the arms extension. Cindy picked up her new reading glasses as well. Afterwards, we enjoyed a nice lunch together. She saw something that I needed and took the time to surprise me. Cindy made me think about what thoughtful act I could do for someone else so that they may be surprised, laugh or just feel good like Cindy did for me."

Peter finished, "I always say that it only takes a minute to be courteous but it requires other-focused thinking. To make others feel special or to go the extra mile is a special mind set. One snowy, Baltimore morning, I arrived early at work to notice that our snow removal contractor, Don, had already plowed our entire driveway. Not only did he plow the driveway but I also noticed that he'd cleared the snow from the awning over our front entrance way. Imagine that—on such a busy night and morning for him, he took time to get out off his truck and clear the snow so it would not fall on our heads."

"Something so small but something most people probably wouldn't do," I nodded. "I always appreciate it when our newspaper delivery man puts the paper on our front porch underneath our deck when it's raining so I don't get wet."

"In observing your actions," I continued, "you have always tried to go above and beyond to help me and others. If a same-day delivery needed to be made from Mid-Atlantic in Baltimore to a customer in Richmond, VA, you drove down to make the delivery. When Krista and I moved to Boulder, we had woefully underestimated how much stuff we had to move, but you helped us by dropping off empty shipping boxes at our apartment, picking up our full boxes and shipping them to us in Boulder."

"After every conversation I have with you," I finished, "you always ask me, 'Is there anything that I can do for you?' It's a simple question, yet sends a powerful message that says to me that this person really cares about me and wants to help me. This person is other-focused."

Chapter 21

Creating an Interdependent Ecosystem

"Dependent people need others to get what they want. Independent people can get what they want through their own effort. Interdependent people combine their own efforts with the efforts of others to achieve their greatest success."
~ Stephen Covey ~

"How does everything tie together?" I asked Peter over the phone. "You've talked about the need for principles, having a vision and goals, and the importance of trust. You've explained how grounded principles enable a business and a person to make better decisions. You've shared how trust is a foundation of a successful culture and strong relationships, whether between individuals or between businesses. We've talked about how leaders influence others in a positive way and the importance of putting processes in place for continuous improvement. Finally, you stressed how being other-focused shows how much a person or business cares. So, how does everything tie together?"

"Think of everything like an ecosystem," answered Peter. "Let me give you an example. During a recent management meeting at Cindy and Bill's house, I spent time admiring their 120-gallon saltwater aquarium that highlights the entire basement area. Like so many things in life, it is easy to take this beautiful display for granted. Behind the scenes of this successful ecosystem, however, are a story and some lessons to be learned and applied to each of our businesses and personal lives."

Peter began his story, "Bill grew up with freshwater aquariums but had always wanted a saltwater tank. As Bill said, anyone can have a saltwater tank with some saltwater fish. Bill's vision was to have a saltwater reef with living coral in the tank. In taking on this challenge, Bill pushed himself out of his own comfort zone. Growth comes from creating new things, and all new things (including visions) are created twice, first mentally then physically."

He continued, "By purchasing some books about saltwater tanks and asking for advice, Bill took the first step up the dark stairs of uncertainty. After getting help with the setup and initial testing of the tank, he was on his own. Bill's weekly tank tasks included tests, data collection and analysis, just like our weekly tasks at Mid-Atlantic. Bill learned about the importance of calcium, alkalinity, nitrates and specific gravity, perhaps the equivalent of cash flow, profit margins, inventory turns and on-time delivery in a business ecosystem like Mid-Atlantic's. He also learned about fish, coral, shrimp and crabs. In the Mid-Atlantic ecosystem, this might be the equivalent to our employees, customers and suppliers. Not all fish are 'reef safe' just as different employees, customers, and suppliers are not compatible with all business environments."

I commented, "This is a good analogy for the principles we've talked about."

Peter said, "An important point to note about a saltwater reef is that every organism in the tank functions interdependently as an ecosystem to keep the coral happy, healthy and alive. Mid-Atlantic's living coral is our customer base. We all function inside the Mid-Atlantic's ecosystem to keep our customers and suppliers happy and healthy."

"Coral is a living animal, but with no skeleton," Peter continued. "It is kept healthy by dosing chemicals, testing and adjusting. Actions and behaviors in both ecosystems need to support the vision and mission that are in place. Fish are selected and added to the reef to provide a certain function, much in the same that we carefully select new employees, new customers, new suppliers and new processes. The hippo fish clears algae since the coral do not like algae; cleaner shrimp jump on to new fish to clean off any parasites that may harm the coral; the clownfish feeds the coral in exchange for the protection it receives from living in the coral. Remember Nemo from *Finding Nemo*? Needless to say, there is no room for predator fish within Bill's or Mid-Atlantic's ecosystems."

"How did Bill choose his fish?" I asked.

Peter said, "Fish selection is never based on emotion but rather by need. Bill explained that because of an emotional purchase, he currently has a fish by the name of Mr. Gobie that has grown too big for the environment. Mr. Gobie eats the small fish and snails and, to make matters worse, Bill cannot catch Mr. Gobie because he hides. Over the years, we have had to purge Mr. Gobie-type employees from Mid-Atlantic's ecosystem."

"Like your salesman?" I asked.

"Yes," replied Peter. "Six months ago, Bill lost his entire reef. The fish were saved but the coral was lost because of a phosphate problem that contaminated the water. Bill had not been checking phosphate levels because he did not know he needed to do so. Bill was ready to give up on living coral and settle with just a saltwater tank with fish. Then Bill remembered his original vision of having a living reef. His persistence kicked in and he learned how to treat the phosphate problem. Bill compares the experience with his tank to Mid-Atlantic not being as close to its customers as it should be. As an example, one of our vendors measures Mid-Atlantic on on-time delivery and recently rated us a poor 85%, not for being late, but for being early. Customers want to minimize inventory because of space constraints and for cash-flow. We were not measuring the impact of our early deliveries."

"That's interesting," I said.

Peter continued, "Bill is very proud of his accomplishment with living coral and has realized that 'the key to the many is the one.' He knows, understands and appreciates each of his fish in the ecosystem. In fact, he has developed special diets for each. Like the fish, Mid-Atlantic employees have special needs and circumstances as well. In the coming months, Bill will be trading coral with other saltwater tank owners in order to add diversity within his saltwater reef. Bill hopes to create a coral wall similar to the ivy wall at Camden Yards."

"That's a nice story," I replied. "When you talk about interdependence, I think about Apple and their system of iPhones, laptops, desktops, iPads and AppleTV. One of the reasons that I like Apple is that all of their products interact with each other. For example, I can make a note about an appointment in my iPhone then get a pop up appointment reminder on my MacBook Air while I'm working on a presentation that I've streamed to our large screen TV."

"That's a great example," said Peter. "Creating an environment where individuals all contribute to the greater cause enables businesses and individuals to thrive."

Chapter 22

Taking a Break

"Adopt the pace of nature: Her secret is patience."
~ Ralph Waldo Emerson ~

I had finished compiling all the stories into what I thought would be our final draft in late 2012. I shared the draft with Peter: "I need your feedback. What do you think?"

I didn't get an answer. We put the book aside for almost two years. Life got in the way.

At first, I was frustrated and disappointed. We had both invested hundreds of hours of time in the book. I felt like I had accomplished nothing because nothing was published.

Peter and I continued to talk over the next two years. Occasionally the topic of the book would come up but we both acknowledged that we were busy with other things and would revisit writing again in the future when life slowed down for both of us.

In the fall of 2014, I received this email from Peter:

Hello David,

After 9 years of competing in the Lake Placid Ironman race, I have joined the "Team For Cures" for a higher purpose to "make it count." It is my goal to use my 2015 race as a fundraiser and platform for the Multiple Myeloma Research Foundation. Supporting the MMRF in their mission to accelerate drug discovery that will lead to a cure is very important and personal to our family. Please help me make a difference in this fight against cancer. Please help me "make it count" as I race again in Lake Placid.

I clicked on the fundraising page and read about Peter's goal to raise $20,000 as part of the MMRF team. What caught my eye was the next to the last paragraph on Peter's fundraising page:

Get a copy of my new book: For contributions of $140.60 (total distance of Ironman triathlon) or more, you will receive a signed copy of my upcoming book when published in December 2015.

I smiled. Peter had set a public goal to publish a book in December 2015, which gave him accountability. We would finish it.

We didn't talk about the book until I flew back to Maryland in May for Krista's brother's wedding. She and I met Peter for breakfast near the airport before the wedding. I hadn't seen Peter in almost a year.

Peter looked the same and we quickly settled into our familiar banter. I could tell Peter was excited to finally finish the book.

"What do you think about the latest draft?" I asked him. "It's been more than two and a half years since we wrote it."

Peter said, "I need to read through it again. There are some new stories that we should add. I want to talk about my retirement from Mid-Atlantic Rubber and transitioning the business management to Bill and Cindy. Because I'm no longer involved much with Mid-Atlantic, it has become even more critical that we finish the book as a place to capture the stories and the history of what makes Mid-Atlantic so unique."

"What's next for you," I asked him, "now that you're no longer working?"

"That's a good question," answered Peter. "I feel like I'm struggling to find my purpose now. Maybe after we finish the book we can use it as a platform to help others. Imagine if I could use the book as a platform for talking to groups of high school or college students. What a difference I could make."

We began writing again.

Chapter 23

Endings Are a Start

"What we call the beginning is often the end. And to make an
end is to make a beginning. The end is where we start from."
~ T.S. Eliot ~

Peter talked about Rudy one day on the phone. Rudy was his twelve pound Yorkshire terrier with diabetes who had recently passed away.

Peter began, "Unlike most dogs, Rudy never saw the inside of a kennel because he went everywhere with us—the beach, staying at the Greenbrier, visiting relatives, racing at Ironman Lake Placid and travels to Naples, Orlando, the Carolina's, Atlanta and even Chicago. Rudy had a lot of personality and lots of names such as: Iron Dog, Porky Yorkie and Gypsy Dog, but none of those names worked when we called him unless he was ready to come. We made a lot of sacrifices for Rudy and spent a lot of money on his health issues but it was all worth it for the unconditional love he gave back. I used to joke that if I were to come home after robbing a bank, Rudy would still wag his tail and kiss me as if I were perfect. Our relationship bank account with Rudy was overflowing."

He continued, "When Rudy died at fourteen years old, he created a void in our hearts. Rudy had been dying slowly for a while but nothing can prepare you for that final goodbye. Everywhere we go now is a reminder of Rudy and how much we miss him. We suddenly had more freedom because we were no longer restricted to the house for his shots and eye drops twice a day, but we lost our purpose taking care of him. I really miss his presence and our daily routine. Kathy cried every day since he died. We are getting on with life after Rudy but it will take time to heal his passing. He is in a much better place and no longer be suffering."

I could feel the sadness choke up in my own chest as I listened to Peter talk. Krista and I had put our Dalmatian, Princess, to sleep after her long battle with back pain. She was also fourteen years old and had passed away in January.

I said, "Listening to you talk about Rudy reminds me of Princess. She had been with me for ten years and had been born deaf. It was really, really tough on Krista and me to watch her health fade so fast. I was the one who finally nodded to the vet to administer the injection as both Krista and I cried as we held her."

"Endings can be tough, but they don't all have to be that way," Peter said. "One of my core beliefs is that happy endings start by proactively planning your happy ending then establishing the priorities to achieve it. Happy endings, whether on TV, at the movies, in the theater or in real life literally make the hair stand up on my arms. I can always tell how much I like a movie or TV show by the ending. I believe all happy endings start with the very things that we have talked about in this book. My retirement story is definitely a happy ending and a personal accomplishment."

"Tell me more," I asked him.

He said, "I learned the importance of vision and goal setting when I was forty years old. Part of the homework was to write down short-range, medium-range and long-range goals. The long-range goals were five to ten years out; they were my dreams. Kathy always says that she is the doer and

I am the dreamer so I loved this vision exercise. My third long-range goal was to retire at age fifty-eight. It was right behind owning my own business and competing in the Ironman in Kona. Go big or go home, right?"

"Interesting," I said. "I didn't realize that you had these dreams for so long. You were really thinking ahead. How did you actually retire from Mid-Atlantic?"

"We ultimately did such a good job at Mid-Atlantic that I literally put myself out of a job. I began traveling more and spending less time in the office. I was making fewer day-to-day decisions and no one was calling me for my advice. I adopted a new title I called the Culture Keeper. It was Mid-Atlantic's principle-centered, other-focused, high-trust, continuous improvement and leadership culture that had enabled the company to move from rust to trust and continue to grow year after year. I didn't need to be present in the office. After all, principles are the boss. I never officially retired from Mid-Atlantic. That's what is so strange to me. I gradually just tiptoed away. I suddenly had freedom but no purpose. I needed a new purpose. Maybe this is a little of what Kathy felt when Katie went off to college. I remember wanting to get back involved with Mid-Atlantic but I thankfully did not."

I said, "I experienced something different when I retired from competing in triathlons. The difference was that I didn't plan to stop racing like you planned to stop leading Mid-Atlantic; I stopped because of burnout. I had lost my drive and motivation. I thought I would take a break for a few months but it's now been five years and I doubt I will ever compete as a triathlete again. But, I am still able to coach and help other triathletes even though I'm not actively racing. I also now have the wisdom of experiencing what happens if athletes continue to train and race too much without listening to their bodies when their bodies badly need the rest. Training in moderation and taking breaks are necessary for long-term success and injury prevention. I share my experiences with my clients so that they don't end up burned out and injured like I did."

Peter said. "That's great that you learned from your mistake in doing too much training and racing and can help others avoid similar pitfalls. That's being other-focused. Your comments make me wonder if it is possible that endings are a necessary part of life, kind of like 'change' and that we can grow depending on how we embrace the event."

Chapter 24

Beginnings

"Do not wait: the time will never be 'just right'.
Start where you stand, and work whatever tools you may have at
your command and better tools will be found as you go along."
~ Napoleon Hill ~

The following week, I asked Peter, "Let's go back to your beginning at Mid-Atlantic when you took over from Clarence. You had never seen Mid-Atlantic before you accepted his job offer. You basically took the job on a promise and a handshake. What was that like?"

Peter answered, "When I joined Mid-Atlantic in in 1989, I didn't have an office and no one knew why I was there or what my responsibility was. Clarence was both the owner of Mid-Atlantic Rubber Company and the sales representative for Olson Wire Products Company. I was at Mid-Atlantic for two years before I was recognized as the General Manager. Having said that, there really were no titles for anyone, even today."

Peter continued, "I remember asking Clarence during my second week at Mid-Atlantic, 'What is one goal that you would like me to accomplish over the next six months?' Clarence replied that he would like to see a computer installed in order to protect and grow the business. His second request was to hire an accountant so that the accounting could be done on-site. We hired Cindy as our accountant first then spent the next six months sourcing and installing our very first computer and distribution software. We selected IBM because of its quality and service reputation. You get what you pay for, right?"

"Yep," I said.

Peter continued, "Over the years, we have upgraded, replaced and customized our hardware and software to match our growth needs. After our employees, our investment in computer hardware and software is the largest and most important asset on our books. We still use IBM today."

"That's a long-term relationship," I commented. "What was it like working with Clarence?"

"Clarence was always hands off and let me do things my way," Peter replied. "Clarence treated me like an owner from my very first day on the job and in later years by gifting me more and more of the business. He also quickly involved me in the sales work at Olson Wire, mentoring me when we made sales calls together. I started the stats report and sent it to him weekly so he did not have to worry about the Mid-Atlantic business and instead could focus 100% of his time on sales for Olson Wire. I helped launch Mid-Atlantic's new company mission around caring for our employees like owners and backed it up with continuous leadership development training for all. We began to create the culture that I had dreamed about for years."

Peter continued, "When Clarence suddenly became ill in 1992, he asked me to make all of his sales calls for him. Olson Wire became half of my twelve-hour workday. I suddenly had two full-time jobs and the stress to go along with it. I remember feeling out of control as I traveled more, gained weight, slept less and felt disconnected from my family. During this period, I was checking in with my body and my emotions and having a tough time mentally and physically. But I remembered my paradigm about what I would do for others if I was given the chance. I made a deal with Clarence to give him $2,000 per month from my commission checks for two years. I continued to do so for five years. It was my way of buying Clarence's sales rep business, a business that meant so much to him until he became sick. He did not need the money, but I am sure he appreciated the gesture. Definitely a win for both of us."

"It's interesting to me how things evolve, especially through unexpected events like illnesses," I said.

"That's very true," said Peter. "Things don't always turn out the way you think they will. In some cases, what looks like a bad situation may be a blessing in disguise. I had never seen my dad so happy as when he came home with Nicki, my stepmom to be. I was fifteen years old and it had been two years since my mom had died. I immediately saw Nicki's white go-go boots and red Chevy Chevelle convertible and thought, 'Way to go, Dad.' Little did I know that this new beginning would be life changing for the years that followed."

He continued, "Before Nicki was in our lives, we kids ate dinner at 5 PM and my parents ate dinner separately later. Nicki introduced family dinners to our home. We all became involved in meal preparation and the cleanup, and we all were expected to eat dinner at the table as a family. Nicki also became the disciplinarian in our family, and I give her all the credit for how well my sister, brothers, and I turned out. Without her courage, love, and discipline, we would have ended up in a much different place. Although it was not always easy for her, raising four teenagers was one of the most purposeful things she did in her life. My stepmom truly cared about each of us and was our leader and my lifesaving coach. She gave our family a much needed new beginning shortly after my mom died."

"That's great that you had such a strong relationship with Nicki," I said. "She seems like a wonderful person."

"I've been thinking about martial arts as a new beginning for me," I continued. "Ever since I was a kid, I had this dream to be a black belt in a martial art that would not only teach me self-defense but also help me develop as a person. When I started the To-Shin Do® style of martial arts in early 2014, I thought I was going to be learning only a fixed series of movements or katas for self-defense. What I've since discovered is that my style of martial arts is all about principles. We learn katas as examples of techniques but ultimately we are learning fundamental principles like good body posture, using gravity instead of muscle and taking our opponent's balance while maintaining our own. The katas help me integrate the principles into movements and actions. If I can get the principles correct, then I don't have to learn a large number of fixed responses. Instead, I can use the principles to defend appropriately against an attacker, whatever the attack may be."

"That's a great example, David," said Peter. "You competed in triathlons for such a long time and you were a very good athlete. You're starting over from scratch with martial arts. That takes courage."

"I'll give you another more recent example of a new beginning," he said. "Shortly after I retired, Kathy and I began talking about moving to a new home with a vision of first-floor living. Our current home was built new in 1989 with the master bedroom and the washer and dryer on the second floor. Our other vision was to downsize, consolidate and donate twenty-five years of 'stuff' that had accumulated in our garage, storage areas, basement and offsite storage. With Katie living in Atlanta and not moving back home, Kathy and I decided that it was time for us to finally tackle what we had been procrastinating for years. 'H2O' became the project name for the second O'Dunne home."

"I like how use acronyms for your plans," I said.

He continued, "Shortly into our downsizing project, we began looking at new homes. We stumbled upon a fifty-five-and-over retirement community only four miles away from our current house and we kept going back to visit the community. That old expression 'When it's right, you'll know it,' fit and we contracted for a new home with a closing date of seven months away. Seven months gave us plenty of time to complete our downsizing and prepare our house for sale."

"Once we had committed," Peter continued, "we were nervous. Did we do the right thing? It's that faith thing again. Start with faith and take one step at a time up the dark staircase. My personal vision for the house was to 'Wow!' Kathy. I wanted her to be so excited about our new home. I also wanted us to do this project together and for her to feel like it was fun. As with any project this size, there were ups and downs, but by breaking the process down into mini goals, we were successful. We worked hard and had fun designing our new home together. We contracted for an outdoor deck and living space six months prior to even moving into the home."

"Continuous improvement before you even moved in?" I asked him.

"Yes," Peter said. "Continuous improvement also applies to a brand new home. Planning ahead turned out to be a really smart idea because the outdoor addition was almost 100% complete by the time we moved into our new home. We both love our new home and we have met so many nice people in our new neighborhood. Other than missing our previous neighbors, we have no regrets about moving. Now when we travel, Kathy tells me that she misses her new home. That says it all."

"As I think about it, there are some common threads between all of your stories," I replied thoughtfully. "You had a vision for what you wanted. You wanted to run a company with a culture that treated people like you wanted to be treated. Your step-mom wanted a cohesive family. You and Kathy wanted to purge and get into a first-floor home. You still want to compete in Kona."

"Yes," replied Peter. "Every vision starts with an initial leap of faith requiring courage followed by sticking with principles, goal setting, planning and building trusting relationships. And don't forget the stumbling blocks and obstacles along the way."

Chapter 25

Leaving a Legacy

"Carve your name on hearts, not tombstones. A legacy is etched
into the minds of others and the stories they share about you."
~ Shannon L. Alder ~

It was early November and we had targeted a completion date of November 30th for the book to be ready for final editing, layout and printing. I wanted another example from Peter to summarize the message that the book was getting across.

"We're in the final stretch," I said to Peter over the phone. "I'm wrapping up the writing and then we will be sending our final draft out to readers for feedback. We have a lot of great examples of things you've accomplished in both your personal life and your career, but can you give me an example of how what you've done has transferred to others?"

Peter answered, "All that we've talked about is directly transferrable to other people and other businesses. That's the magic of it all. I'll give you an example that has made me very proud as a father."

Peter explained how Katie was a cross-country runner in high school and throughout college. She was not the fastest runner, but she was the only senior in college who raced all four years despite the pressures of her studies and a very demanding coach. When Katie graduated, she decided to take up triathlons to add some cross-training to her fitness regimen.

Peter said, "Katie was a little rusty on the bike in 2012 when she did her very first triathlon, the Ocean City Beach Patrol Triathlon. I remember exiting the water behind her and seeing her mount her bike with her swim cap still on and no helmet. I yelled and signaled to her. After removing her swim cap and clipping on her helmet, Katie remounted her bike only to fall down. I could see that she was hurt, but she got back on her bike and finished the race."

I reflected on my own experience leaving the transition area to start the run with a bike helmet still on my head.

Peter continued, "Katie left for graduate school a few weeks later, taking the triathlon bug with her to Atlanta. She spent the next three years improving her swim, bike, and run. She joined a masters team for swimming, a Spinning® club for biking and hired a coach for running and nutrition. She also joined a local triathlon racing team called Podium Sports. She raced, she trained and she studied; she improved and improved and improved. Katie started finishing on the podium in most of her races. At a USA Triathlon Regional Championship race, she qualified for the National Championship where she raced and qualified for the World Championships in Chicago, only three years after her first triathlon."

"That's impressive," I commented.

"How did Katie do it?" Peter asked. "She did what all great leaders do. She took total responsibility for herself and her surroundings. She set her vision. She was principle-centered. She was disciplined, focused and made lots of sacrifices. She rarely missed a workout and she never let her grades suffer either, graduating with a 3.9 GPA. Katie had created a healthy and productive lifestyle for herself, a culture, not unlike the culture we created at Mid-Atlantic."

"That's awesome," I said. "Can you give an example of what's going on at Mid-Atlantic now that you're gone and no one is calling you to ask questions?"

Peter answered, "Last year, a new employee was hired for the Cash-Flow Team and our entire computer hardware and software were upgraded. Sound familiar? It was déjà vu again with Cindy being hired and our first computer purchase with the same reason to protect and grow the business. However, the decision making, approval, and implementation came from the current leadership team and not from me."

He continued. "I recently stopped by the office to see Bill and noticed that the lighting was different; it was brighter. When I asked Bill, he said that the Warehouse Team had identified some dimly lit areas in the warehouse, a problem that didn't absolutely need be fixed, but it was fixed because it would make the warehouse more pleasant for the team. Bill went one step further and hired a vendor to design, layout and install more than 100 new lighting fixtures using CFLs and LED bulbs with twenty-year lives throughout the entire building. The decision to replace the old, inefficient lighting with new, brighter and more efficient lighting was a great way to plan for the future. The utility company paid for 85% of the upgrade cost and the savings in maintenance and bulb replacement will yield significant savings in the years to come."

"That must feel good," I commented. "You're no longer there, but the culture you established continues without you. You've left a legacy."

Peter replied, "Leadership means getting results as well as developing the next generation of leaders. Clarence was a great leader and model for me and I have been a great leader and model for others. The current generation of leaders at Mid-Atlantic Rubber is continuing the legacy started by Clarence. You reap what you sow and you often get back much more than what you give out."

Chapter 26

Winning the Race

Leaves are prancing here and there,
dancing near and everywhere.
All the children gather 'round
raking leaves without a sound.
Animals all collecting food for the winter coming soon.
Fathers carry great big logs,
getting ready for the wind's great song.
Everybody being so busy,
never stops and it's a pity.
They never get to see the colors,
that blend together like no others.
And no one ever stops and sees
the intricate weaving of the breeze.
For no one ever takes the time
to see the season soaring by.
"Autumn" by Katie O'Dunne

Peter and I were nearing completion of the book. He shared Katie's poem "Autumn" with me and said, "You can look at something one hundred times and see the same thing. It's only when you think differently and try to see things differently that you experience growth. This poem speaks to many themes in the book: changing your paradigms, doing the opposite of what others do, living each day to the fullest and not taking life for granted. Embracing change just like the change of seasons. Nature itself is based on principles such as growth. We can not change the order of the seasons nor can we change the weather on race day. We can adjust to it. Adjust our attitude, our clothing choices, maybe even our wheel selection."

"It's been quite a journey to write this book," I said. "In the beginning, I didn't imagine that writing the book would be a story in itself. You've helped me in many areas of my life and, perhaps most importantly, have encouraged me, especially when I didn't know I needed encouragement. You've also helped me to look at things differently and convinced me that things will work out if I stick with my principles."

"For me," replied Peter, "training for an Ironman is a metaphor for my life. It's a project and a goal that I work on all year long. And yes, there's my never-ending dream to qualify for Kona. Ironman training helps keep me healthy and confident, but it also keeps me grounded to principles that I am able to use in my professional and personal life. Principles like planning, preparation, hard work, sacrifice and maintaining a positive attitude. More than anything, the training and racing has taught me that success is what you determine it to be and being successful comes from being principle-centered and focusing on those things you can do something about."

He continued, "My triathlon journey began with my vision to compete in the Ironman World Championship in Kona. I began taking the first step when I met Jonathan and signed up for my first Ironman. A few years later when I met you, we discussed goals and came up with an annual plan to achieve them. You then created detailed weekly plans for me and coached me through several training and racing seasons. We learned to trust each other, which enabled us to communicate openly with each other and work through the obstacles like my hamstring injuries and challenges like travel for work, that interrupted my training routine and diet. You also encouraged and believed in me, always focusing on the positive of what I could do."

He added, "If you think about it, training accounts for 96% of the time while racing counts for only about 4%—that's more than 540 of training for only 22 hours of racing each year."

"Yep, it's a lot of work upfront and things didn't always go smoothly," I said. "When you tore your hamstring, the doctor told you that you wouldn't be able to run for a long period of time. You were in pain and unable to train effectively, yet you were the eternal optimist. I could feel your frustration when I talked with you but you never voiced a complaint or blamed anyone but yourself. You were focused on looking for a way to make your leg better so you could move on."

"It was tough for me," Peter admitted. "With the injury, I didn't even know if and when I'd be able to run again. My goals had to change. My paradigm shifted from training for an Ironman to simply being able to run again. The injury was a big bump on the road of life."

"Yet, I had my principles, values and mission to fall back on," he continued. "I focused on the things I could influence; the things that I could do something about. I couldn't run, but I could see a physical therapist for rehabilitation and strengthen my legs to prevent the injury from happening again."

I added, "I've noticed that qualifying for Ironman Hawaii seems to attract two types of people. The first type only likes the idea of going to Kona, so they fall short on the commitment and discipline, especially when the training becomes difficult and prolonged. The second type does the work while acquiring the necessary knowledge and skills to be successful. Most people with your injury or your other commitments would call it quits early on and move on to something else."

"Do the opposite of what most others would do," said Peter. "When I was running this past Sunday, I remember the hills and thought how much I both dislike and like the hills. The same is true with the wind when I'm biking, and my favorite challenges on the swim are the currents and waves. These three obstacles from a different perspective, or paradigm, are character builders. They are training tools that help me improve performance. When you're going through the biggest obstacles in life, your obstacles define you."

I nodded affirmatively. I knew all about obstacles on a triathlon course.

"I love race week," Peter said. "It's the opportunity to break personal records, try out new strategies, test new equipment and push myself both physically and mentally. Everything miraculously seems to come together by race day. I credit this to the fact that I've had great coaches and trainers (my secret weapons) who have prepared me every day of every week for race day. It really is all about training and preparation regardless of your passion or profession. My coaching and personal training team designed programs that brought me to the start line healthy and confident. Now it's up to me to design my race day plan and execute."

He continued, "Picture the swim start at Ironman Lake Placid with more than 2,000 athletes lined up in the water on the lakeshore. It's quite an impressive sea of colored swim caps as all the athletes crowd in close together in the water to wait for the starting gun to go off."

"Yes," I replied. "I remember the swim start at Lake Placid well. When the gun goes off, it's instant chaos as everyone surges forward stroking and kicking to fight for position."

"Then comes the bike," Peter continued. "Sometimes the wind will be in my face and sometimes it will be at my back, so it's really all about my attitude. I keep my head down into the headwind and remember that there will be a tailwind at the turnaround. I don't focus on the finish line but, like in the swim, I pick mini milestones like the next aid station or the end of the first lap to get me to the end of the bike leg. Towards the second half of the bike, the pain begins to set in. For me, it starts in the butt and continues to the legs. From this point on, every mile now seems like two miles. I just could not wait to get off the bike."

"Yep," I said, "The bike leg in an Ironman is tough because it's so long. It's hard to stay focused."

"Then there's the run," he said.

"As you know, it requires reaching deep within oneself to finish the race." "The run is where the rubber hits the road. Sorry, I could not resist. The run starts off as a slow walk, then a slow run. At the midway point of the run, some runners are going into the finishing oval to cross the finish line but I still have 13.1 miles left to go. My mental toughness kicks in. Every step in painful. I try to run a little to pass the next walker. Walk, run, walk run. Then I see my family, and I know that 3 miles is nothing."

I remembered the pain from my own Ironman runs.

He continued, " During each race, I cannot control the weather or the water temperature, but I can control my clothing choices, my nutrition plan, and most important, my attitude. I can put brand new tires and tubes on my bike to minimize the chance for flat tires. I can ride safely and aware during the race to avoid penalties and crashes. I can taper my training on race week so that I have a fresh body on race day. I can hydrate and get lots of sleep during race week."

"But," he added, "If you think about it, each race is not just about you or me. Each race is about each individual's own challenges and journey to be there on race day and achieve success."

"How so?" I asked.

Peter replied, "We're a small club of endurance athletes each with different reasons for competing and different stories of how we arrived at the start-ing line. Every athlete has different goals for the race. I applaud the 70+ year-old runner that always seems to pass me at every Ironman race I have done. I want every athlete to finish before the cut-off time. I start each race in the water shaking hands with the person on my left and my right and wish them good luck. If I see someone with a flat on the bike, I ask if they need anything. It only takes a second to be courteous. It's an abundance mentality that we can all win. In triathlon, just like in life, we have to do things in progression. We take our vision and big goals and break them down into smaller, more manageable pieces. It's how we deal with the cur-rents or the waves during the swim leg. We focus on what we're doing in the moment and stop worrying so much about the future. We'll get there soon enough."

"So what happens at the end of the race" I asked him. "What do you feel? What's going through your mind?"

He replied, "David, I always win my race. The finish line, an act of service, helping a friend or complimenting someone who has helped me is really about peace of mind. I want to be able look at myself in the mirror and be happy with myself. I want to sleep well at night knowing that I have trusting relationships and that I have unlimited potential to do and accomplish so much more by helping others find their uniqueness, challenge their paradigms and exceed their self-imposed limiting thoughts."

Peter concluded, "My finish line celebration is with my family, friends and coach. Many people are doing their own Ironman race whether it's battling a health problem, coping with a job loss or working through a relationship issue. Effectiveness in life is all about healthy relationships with oneself and with others. Leadership is about helping others to find their voice after you have found your own voice. You are finding your voice as an athlete, coach, author, entrepreneur and maybe something else that you haven't quite discovered."

"So when you will qualify for Kona?" I asked.

He replied, "Ironman has a legacy program that you can apply to compete at Kona if you have done twelve Ironmans and are currently signed up for a race. I meet all the qualifications, but I really want to qualify on my own. I am always so inspired by the athletes in their seventies who pass me on the bike. I want to continue Ironman racing into my seventies. I plan to qualify for Kona at Lake Placid in 2018."

I believe Peter will do just that.

Epilogue

*"Some people come into our lives and quickly go. Some stay for a while and
leave footprints on our hearts. And we are never, ever the same."*
~ Anonymous ~

Peter's stories have been captured and the writing is done, closing out this
journey that Peter and I started together in 2010. Throughout his life, Peter
has affected many, many others in meaningful ways as shown in the stories
we've shared. With this book, he now has the opportunity to affect many,
many more people.

What is the Peter effect? Peter's daughter, Katie, summarized it best at his
60th birthday party:

> It's been pretty amazing to come up and see my dad on his 60th
> birthday.
>
> I remember his 50th birthday. I remember being at the baseball game
> when I was fifteen. I was happy to be there but I preferred being

consumed with a lot of other teenager stuff—texting my friends and whomever I liked at the time.

I think I really loved and cared about my dad then but it took me another ten years to really realize what an incredible person my dad is.

I think of all of the things that come to me now, I think of triathlon after watching my dad, growing up and seeing how cool that was my dad was doing that.

The things my dad did in the church. I'm in ministry now. Just the hard work that my dad did.

I remember being at Mid-Atlantic and having people come up and say, "Your dad changed my life in some way." I know everyone says something like that, but it really means something to me now.

I brag about you all the time. I don't know if you know that but at work I'm always talking about my dad and how I'm doing this because my dad said this or I'm teaching these kids the 7 Habits because my dad said "These are what's important."

Everything that I am is because of the person my dad was and how he raised me and I am really, really thankful for that.

Peter's Key Points

If Peter could summarize everything in this book as key points, they would be these:

1. Treat others as I would like to be treated—the golden rule. And even better is to treat others the way they want to be treated—the platinum rule.

2. You get what you pay for.

3. Things are not always what they seem to be. Check your paradigms. Don't be afraid to change your paradigms if they are outdated.

4. Strive for win-win. Ask what's a win for the other person before you think about a win for you

5. Enjoy and expect great customer service. Give feedback.

6. Always strive for the very best possible.

7. Live each day to the fullest and do not take life for granted.

8. Happy endings start by being proactive to plan your happy ending then establishing priorities to achieve it.

9. Maintain a positive attitude no matter what happens. Be optimistic. Things have a way of working out for the best.

10. Be a "people-person" first. Leaders love people. See the best in others and help others.

11. Honesty is always the best policy. Have a reputation for being trustworthy.

12. Work hard and success will come.

13. Lead by example. Be a great role model. Someone is always watching you.

14. Be a good sport. Winning isn't everything.

15. The past does not equal the future.

16. There is always a way. Never say never.

17. Don't prejudge others by their looks or their behavior.

18. It only takes a second to be courteous.

19. Give unconditionally and you will receive. Make deposits regularly to the key people in your life.

20. Every employee deserves to be led by a great leader.

21. Always do what you say you will do. Keep commitments and promises. Expect the same in return.

22. You will perform your best and feel good about yourself when healthy.

23. Engage with others. Most problems can be solved by those around you.

24. Obstacles, failures and hard times help to form your core.

25. You can have it all if you help enough others get what they want.

26. For huge monumental changes in your life, work on your paradigms.

27. A culture of trust is the quickest way to profit. Create a high-trust culture in all areas of your life.

28. Money is important but purpose, contribution and feeling like an owner are the keys to success in business.

29. People are capable of doing so much more if they have the right culture and the right coach.

30. Be a good listener. Listen to understand not to reply.

31. Find your uniqueness and make it your purpose.

32. Help others to find their uniqueness, gifts and talents.

33. Continue to improve yourself on all dimensions with goals and initiatives that are meaningful.

34. Avoid becoming obsessed with anything.

35. Follow principles of success. Do things others would not do. Figure out what everyone else does and do the opposite. Principles are the boss.

36. Make good choices daily.

37. Take charge of your life. Be a leader and run your life like a successful business.

38. Do things for which there is no penalty for not doing.

39. Create a process for important things in your life.

40. Take twenty minutes to plan your week. Connect with your mission, roles and goals.

41. Growth comes from change. Get out of your comfort zone and watch the impact on yourself and others.